THE
PENINSULA
CAMPAIGN
1862

THE PENINSULA CAMPAIGN 1862

McClellan & Lee
STRUGGLE FOR RICHMOND

Joseph P. Cullen

BONANZA BOOKS · NEW YORK

This is for Babe, who lived and died in the Watt House on the Gaines's Mill battlefield

Contents

List of Maps
and Illustrations

Acknowledgments

The author is indebted to the Virginia State Library, which furnished all the illustrations for this book, and particularly to Mrs. Katherine M. Smith, who was most helpful and cooperative. All the maps have been taken from *Battles and Leaders of the Civil War*, edited by Robert Underwood Johnson and Clarence Clough Buel, 4 vols., New York, 1884–87. In addition, to his good friend and teacher over the years, Mr. J. Ambler Johnston of Richmond, who probably has forgotten more about the battles around Richmond than he will ever know, the author owes more than he can ever repay.

11

Introduction

The American Civil War was unique in many respects. Simultaneously, it was the last of the old wars and the first of the new. It was a war for which neither side had planned and for which neither side was prepared. It was, as Walt Whitman so aptly stated, "a strange, sad war."

With the firing on Fort Sumter, South Carolina in April, 1861 all efforts to find a peaceful solution to the differences between the North and the South ceased. Neither side, however, was anxious to mount an offensive. If the South could not secede from the Union peacefully, then it was determined to defend every acre of territory and maintain its independence to the last. As Confederate President Jefferson Davis proclaimed: "All we ask is to be left alone." With this philosophy there was nothing to be gained by invading the North. Rather, the South wanted to exploit the advantages of defensive operations, which would require fewer men and allow it to use its interior, or shorter, lines of communication and supply to best advantage.

The North, however, would have to assume the offensive if it was determined to prevent secession and carry out President Abraham Lincoln's objective of preserving the Union. To accomplish this, the South would have to be invaded and conquered, which would require large armies, long lines of communications, immense quantities of supplies, and the control of the seaports and rivers of the South. This meant a military effort on a vast scale.

The Federal overall strategy for this unprecedented effort called for a naval blockade of Southern ports to shut off foreign supplies, control of the Mississippi River in order to split the Confederacy on an east-west axis, and a swing through Georgia to split it again on a north-south axis. This was to be the overall strategy and the major Federal offensive, but circumstances dictated otherwise, although in the end control of the Mississippi was the decisive element that eventually doomed the Confederacy. The proximity of the two capitals at Richmond and Washington, a scant 100 miles apart, decreed that major fighting in the East would be continuous throughout the war, and that Virginia would be the war's most constant and bloodiest battleground.

Although the Federal strategy would prove to be correct, the people of the North were too impatient at the start to allow the major emphasis to be given to the war in the West. "On to Richmond" was the cry from the beginning. It was believed that with the fall of the Confederate capital, the Confederacy would quickly collapse. So for four years Richmond remained the primary military objective in the East. The war in the West would be waged simultaneously, although on a reduced scale in the beginning, with its objective of splitting the Confederacy geographically by control of the rivers.

This, then, is the story of the Peninsula Campaign of 1862, the first real professional attempt to capture Richmond and end the war, which saw the emergence of the South's great general and leader, Robert E. Lee, and the emergence and decline of the North's great hope, General George B. McClellan.

Richmond: Linchpin of Strategy for North and South

On the morning of March 17, 1862 the old brick town of Alexandria, Virginia on the outskirts of Washington was crowded with curious spectators gazing in awe at the huge fleet which jammed the Potomac River off the shabby wharves and warehouses. Over 400 ships of all types—steam vessels, brigs, schooners, sloops, ferryboats, barges—were assembled there to transport the Army of the Potomac, over 100,000 strong, down the river, then across Chesapeake Bay to Fort Monroe at the tip of the peninsula between the York and the James rivers on the Virginia coast. Under a pale, winter sun the first regiments of blue-clad troops embarked with bands blaring, flags flying, and three days' cooked rations in their haversacks. In the next three weeks these vessels transported, in addition to the troops, 3,600 wagons, 700 ambulances, 300 pieces of artillery, 2,500 head of cattle, and more than 25,000 horses and mules to Fort Monroe.

Federal Transports on the Potomac

At last a major Federal move against Richmond, capital of
Virginia and the Confederate States of America, was under way.
It had been a long time coming and much was expected from it.
After all, this was the largest amphibious operation the modern
world had ever seen. General Rufus Ingalls, quartermaster general, could truthfully report: "Operations so extensive and important as the rapid and successful embarkation of such an army,
with all its vast equipment, its transfer to the peninsula, and its
supply while there, had scarcely any parallel in history, and certainly none in our country."

Major General George B. McClellan, commander of this best-
trained, -equipped, and -supplied army in American history, embarked with his staff on April 1. As the steamer pushed its way out
into the muddy river, he heaved a sigh of relief. "Officially
speaking," he wrote his wife, "I feel very glad to get away from
that sink of iniquity. . . ."

A strange remark, perhaps, but then McClellan was a strange
man in many respects. When he reported to President Abraham
Lincoln in Washington in July, 1861, he had been welcomed as a
conquering hero, the man who would save the demoralized army.

And demoralized it was. After the firing on Fort Sumter, South Carolina by the Confederates in April, which opened the war, Lincoln had called for 75,000 volunteers. As these raw recruits had poured into Washington in the spring and early summer, the pressure had mounted for a quick invasion of the South. "On to Richmond" was the cry. Under this pressure, Lincoln had ordered General Irvin McDowell to take the field. When McDowell protested that he needed more time to train his troops, Lincoln told him, "You are green, it is true, but they are green also."

There were two main avenues of approach to Richmond: the direct overland approach through Fredericksburg and the approach by water to the tip of the peninsula and then up the peninsula to the capital city. In the summer of 1861 it was decided to use the overland approach. Straight across this road to Richmond lay Manassas, a small railroad settlement a few miles east of the Bull Run mountains. Here Confederate General P. G. T. Beauregard blocked the road with about 22,000 men, while General Joseph E. Johnston commanded a smaller force of about 11,000 at Winchester in the Shenandoah Valley. And here, on July 21, McDowell had led his 35,000 Federal troops on their way to Richmond.

In this first major engagement of the Civil War the Federal army had suffered disaster in a nightmare battle of mistakes fought by poorly trained officers and men. It was routed from the field and retreated in disorder and panic. No longer an army, the frightened soldiers had streamed into Washington by the thousands, a confused mob with no semblance of order or discipline. For miles the roads leading into the city were strewn with the paraphernalia of war—caps, coats, blankets, muskets, canteens, haversacks. Muddy, hungry and foot-sore, they staggered through the streets begging food and buying liquor, dropping in exhaustion on porches, lawns, and sidewalks. Many of the officers, completely demoralized, filled the hotel barrooms and cheap saloons. "The capture of Washington seems now to be inevitable," wrote Edwin M. Stanton, soon to be appointed Secretary of War. "The route, overthrow, and utter demoralization of the whole army is complete."

Thus it was evident that a strong hand was needed to save the capital and bring order out of chaos, and when the president appointed McClellan to supersede McDowell, Washington and the people of the North were relieved.

Shortly before the disaster at Manassas McClellan had defeated a small contingent of Rebels in western Virginia; so his name had the aura of action and victory about it. From his dispatches and newspaper reports, the people had come to believe that a great victory had been achieved. McClellan convinced his soldiers they had "annihilated two armies," and in the process convinced the government and the people because the government and the people wanted to be convinced. The government desperately needed a military leader and the people wanted a hero, a Man on Horseback—and the mantle fell on George B. McClellan.

And for a time it seemed to fit. Everything he had ever tried had been successful. Entering West Point at the age of fifteen by special permission, he graduated second in a class of fifty-nine in 1846. Brevetted twice for gallantry in the Mexican War, in 1855 he won an appointment as an Army observer in the Crimean War, an experience which greatly influenced his later military career. He resigned from the Army in 1857 with the rank of captain to become chief engineer of the Illinois Central Railroad. Shortly thereafter he was promoted to vice-president. At the outbreak of the war he was president of the eastern division of the Ohio and Mississippi Railroad. In 1860 he married Ellen Marcy, daughter of an Army colonel, beating his West Point roommate, Ambrose P. Hill, in the race for her affections. Success seemed to come to him easily and quickly.

He even looked the part. A heavy-set, short, broad-chested man with a thick reddish moustache, he bestrode his horse like a conquering hero, issued commands with an authoritative air, published bombastic proclamations in the style of Napoleon, and put his right hand inside his coat whenever he was photographed and gazed at the camera with a stern, military look. One Massachusetts recruit believed "he looked like a man that was not afraid of the cry On to Richmond. . . ."

McClellan and Wife

Comparisons with Napoleon were inevitable. Correspondents called him Little Mac, the Young Napoleon, Boy Wonder (he was not yet thirty-five years of age). Washington observers noted that he had an "indefinable air of success about him," that "he looked like one who always had succeeded and always will succeed." He seemed assured, self-possessed, radiating confidence with an aura of romantic greatness. In all of Washington only a foreigner, the astute William Howard Russell of the London *Times*, seemed to have any doubts about McClellan. "I like the man," he wrote, "but I do not think he is equal to his occasion or his place."

A close scrutiny of the records of McClellan's subordinate officers might have given others some doubts, too. While the general's proclamation declared that he had "annihilated two armies," the reports showed he had killed less than 300 and captured only about 1,000 of the enemy. The reports also indicated that while subordinate generals W. S. Rosecrans and Jacob D. Cox had successfully carried out their flanking missions, McClellan had bungled his frontal assault, with the result that the remainder of the Confederate force had escaped unharmed. In his official report McClellan underestimated the forces opposed to his subordinate officers and overestimated those opposed to him, so as to leave no doubt that the credit was his. Cox, in his memoirs, on the other hand, stated that in this early campaign McClellan showed characteristics that were later to prove disastrous. "There was the same overestimate of the enemy, the same tendency to interpret unfavorably the sights and sounds in front, the same hesitancy to throw in his whole force when he knew that his subordinate was engaged."

But after the fiasco of Manassas no one was concerned with the past—it was the future that mattered, and for that hope was needed. McClellan gave the North that hope. "I find myself in a new and strange position here," he wrote. "President, Cabinet, Gen. Scott, and all deferring to me. By some strange operation of magic I seem to have become the power of the land." It is revealing to note that in his mind he had become "the" power, not "a" power.

In reality, of course, Manassas had not been the disaster it was generally considered to be. It was, in fact, a blessing in disguise for the North, for it shook the government out of its complacency. "We have undertaken to make war without in the least knowing how," a Washington observer noted. "We have made a false start and we have discovered it. It only remains to start afresh." Now the politicians realized that all the powerful resources of the North would have to be organized and directed in preparation for a long, hard struggle. And the war was not going to be won by the theatrical heroics of untrained three-months volunteers and comic opera officers. A larger army would have to be raised, trained, and equipped, with the enlistments for three years or the duration, not three months. Washington would have to be adequately protected against the slightest chance of capture, for if the capital fell there would be no United States as such.

The army and the defense of Washington would be McClellan's job—a job for which he was brilliantly suited.

Shortly after his arrival, McClellan stated: "I have Washington perfectly quiet now . . . I have restored order very completely already." And indeed he had. The hotels, barrooms, and streets had been emptied of drunken officers and soldiers absent without leave; a rigid system of passes had been promulgated; and regular patrols of the city had been instituted. The bright greens and colorful reds of various militia regiments disappeared, to be replaced by the standard Union blue. The lackadaisical encampments of the volunteers began to assume the orderly look of regular army camps, and drills, reviews, and guard mountings were formal, everyday affairs, with all orders given by bugle calls. One Connecticut volunteer wrote about the new look. "Troops, tents, the frequent thunder of guns practicing, lines of heavy baggage wagons, at reveille and tattoo the air filled with the near and distant roll of drums and the notes of innumerable bugles—all the indications of an immense army, and yet no crowding, no rabble."

Day by day, as the new regiments streamed into Washington, the capital took on the appearance of a huge armed camp, white tents spreading for miles over the surrounding hills, valleys, and riverbanks, the streets echoing to the roll of drums and the call of bugles. Earthen forts were quickly thrown up and soon completely encircled the city in a vast and complicated system of entrenchments. Herds of cattle plodded through the muddy streets to the army commissaries; thousands of horses and mules filled the corrals. From 50,000 in July, the army grew to 168,000 in November, the largest volunteer citizen army in history, and McClellan proudly named it the Army of the Potomac. He reorganized the staff and made his father-in-law, Colonel Randolph B. Marcy, his chief of staff. This was a new position in American military circles. McClellan had learned the value of it in his Crimean experience, and in this respect he was far ahead of any other general in America, North or South. "They give me my way in everything," he exclaimed, "full swing and unbounded confidence. All tell me that I am held responsible for the fate of the nation, and that all its resources shall be placed at my disposal."

While he marshaled and drilled the raw recruits into an efficient fighting machine, orders totaling millions of dollars went out to the factories, mills, forges and foundries, for the huge mass of supplies and equipment that filled the warehouses and lined the camps. And through it all McClellan himself, radiating confidence, dashing through the streets on his great black charger, Daniel Webster, followed by his large and colorful personal staff, with reporters trailing along behind. With this powerful weapon he was forging, and with him to guide and use it, the war would soon be over, or so it seemed. The people and the government were full of confidence.

And yet there were those who wondered why McClellan did not live out in the field across the Potomac with his men, instead of in a house on the northwest corner of Jackson Square. They realized, of course, that this gave him the opportunity to be continually galloping through the streets with his colorful retinue on his way to or from the field, and as he was already being talked about as the next president, it certainly didn't hurt his chances to be seen in all his glory. Russell thought differently, however. He believed McClellan should have been out with his army living among his generals to get to know their strengths and weaknesses, but "faction and intrigue are the cancer which peculiarly eat into the body politic of republics," he wrote, "and McClellan fears, no doubt, that his absence from the capital, even though he went but across the river, would animate his enemies to undermine and supplant him."

Although there is no evidence that anyone was trying to supplant McClellan at this early date, there is abundant evidence to prove McClellan was doing his best to undermine and supplant his immediate superior, old General Winfield Scott, hero of the Mexican War, and now a brevet lieutenant general commanding the United States Army. Since the general was seventy-five years old and plagued with increasing infirmities, it was merely a question of time until he would be retired. But the Young Napoleon was impatient. Two weeks after his arrival in Washington he was complaining that the "old general always comes in the way. He understands nothing, appreciates nothing." He believed that Scott was "the great obstacle" to all his plans.

In a way, of course, McClellan was right. This war had already passed the old hero by. Blinded by the dreams of his past victories in other wars, he wanted to keep the organization of the army as it had always been, in geographic departments, with the largest unit a brigade. He could not visualize divisions, corps, and armies; so McClellan became more and more disrespectful and argumentative, and proceeded to circumvent him in every way possible. The old general was no longer just an obstacle in his path, McClellan declared, he was now the "most dangerous antagonist I have." (Even more dangerous than the Confederate Army at Manassas, apparently.) By August 9 he was confident that "tomorrow the question will probably be decided by giving me absolute control independently of him." But the Boy Wonder had reckoned without President Lincoln.

To the American people generally, Scott was still the great hero. Europe might boast of Napoleon and Wellington, but America had its Washington and Scott, and the feelings of the people could not be ignored completely, at least not by the politicians. Lincoln was genuinely fond of old "Fuss and Feathers," as his subordinates called him, relied upon him for military advice, and was loath to request his retirement. But McClellan finally forced his hand.

Early in October the President called a meeting of several cabinet members and both McClellan and Scott. When the old general could not say how many troops were in and about Washington because McClellan had not informed him, the meeting broke up on a sour note. Scott then turned angrily on McClellan. "You were called here by my advice. When I proposed that you should come here to aid, not supersede, me, you had my friendship and confidence. You still have my confidence." Lincoln was visibly disturbed but still did not act; so McClellan went around his commander in chief and on October 25 met in secret with three Radical Republican senators—Wade, Trumbull, and Chandler—all influential members of the Radical Committee on the Conduct of the War. Scott was for inaction and the defensive, McClellan told them, while he wanted action and one quick campaign to crush the Rebels. That night he wrote his wife that the senators would "make a desperate effort tomorrow to have General Scott retired at once."

Within a week Scott wrote his request for retirement and Lincoln reluctantly accepted it. McClellan exulted. "At last I am the major-general commanding the army."

But as the cool, crisp November days passed, when the blue mists folded over the yellow-spotted hills and scarlet woodlands, and McClellan's army was still marching and drilling and reviewing, there were murmurs of surprise. The Army of the Potomac was spoken of as the largest, best-trained, best-equipped in the world, and people began to wonder why it didn't move when the Rebels had an army of only about 50,000 under Johnston at Manassas, just a two days' march away. Then when the men settled into winter quarters in December, the surprise turned to exasperation, confusion, and suspicion. Earlier, McClellan had promised the Speaker of the House prompt action. "I have no intention of putting the army into winter quarters," he had assured him. "I mean the campaign will be short, sharp, and decisive." He had convinced the Committee on the Conduct of the War, as well as the President and the cabinet, that only Scott's interference held him back. Now Scott was gone and the government and the people were becoming impatient. Lincoln was quoted as saying, "McClellan is a great engineer, but has a special talent for a stationary engine." To Mrs. Lincoln, McClellan was a man who "talks so much and does so little."

With the old general out of the way, McClellan soon found other reasons for not moving. He had appointed a friend of his,

Allan Pinkerton, to his staff as chief of intelligence. An energetic Scotchman, Pinkerton had founded one of the first private detective agencies in the country in Chicago, and it was mainly his reports that had alarmed the government in the so-called Baltimore plot to assassinate Lincoln the previous February. Both he and his operators seemed to believe that they earned their pay by giving exaggerated reports. Now he was reporting to McClellan that the Confederate forces at Manassas far outnumbered the Federal forces, and McClellan believed these reports because he wanted to believe them. "I am here in a terrible place," he told his wife, "the enemy have from three to four times my force," and under those conditions he had no intention of moving if he could possibly avoid it.

Shortly after his arrival in Washington he had written a memorandum to the president giving his ideas on how the war should be conducted. In it he had called for a force of 273,000 for his own army, but only 20,000 for a proposed movement down the Mississippi River. (He explained to his wife: "The real fighting must be here; that in Kentucky will be a mere bagatelle.") He also urged that the railroads leading from Memphis to the east be seized. "The possession of those roads," he informed the president, "in connection with the movement on the Mississippi, would go far towards determining the evacuation of Virginia by the rebels." Evacuate to where? To the west? If so, Lincoln must have wondered why McClellan would need 273,000 troops while only 20,000 would be needed in the west. A short time later, though, McClellan changed his estimate. He now informed the Secretary of War that the Army of the Potomac should number "not less than 300,000 men." When General Sherman suggested an army of 75,000 to carry on the war in the west, McClellan exclaimed indignantly, "The man is crazy."

Early in December a delegation of congressmen called on the president to see what could be done to get the Army of the Potomac in motion. The president defended McClellan and told them the general undoubtedly knew his business, but underneath Lincoln was worried, confused, and sick at heart. He knew he had to keep all the political factions at least reasonably united and that he had to prevent the European powers from recognizing the

Confederacy, but with no military action to back him up this was becoming ever more difficult. Now it was December, Congress was in session, and the pressure to get McClellan moving or replace him was mounting day by day. To the observant Russell, the president was a man "to be pitied; trying with all his might to understand strategy, naval warfare, big guns, the movements of troops, military maps, reconnaissances, occupations, interior and exterior lines, and all the technical details of the art of slaying. He runs from one house to another, armed with plans, papers, reports, recommendations, sometimes good-humored, never angry, occasionally dejected, and always a little fussy." And, in the meantime, "McClellan is still reviewing, and the North are still waiting for victories and paying money. . . ."

In December, too, McClellan fell ill with typhoid fever and as yet no one, including the president, seemed to know what he planned to do or when he planned to do it. Although others could visit him, Lincoln was denied admittance to the sick room. This was nothing new, to be sure, because for several months McClellan had been openly avoiding or snubbing his commander in chief. In desperation the president on January 10 called an emergency meeting of the Secretaries of War and Treasury, and Generals McDowell and Franklin, in an attempt to find out what, if anything, could be done. McDowell proposed an overland movement into Virginia against the Confederate forces at Manassas, while Franklin suggested a movement against Richmond up the York River, but no decision was reached.

Two nights later the same group met again, augmented by Postmaster General Blair, a West Pointer and friend of McClellan, when suddenly the Young Napoleon appeared. The anxious president then told him, in effect, that he had better tell them what his plans were. At this McClellan bristled and refused to discuss any proposed movements of the army. "No general commanding an army would willingly submit his plans to the judgement of such an assembly," he declared, "in which some were incompetent to form a valuable opinion, and others incapable of keeping a secret." This was even more insulting than most of those present could have realized, because McClellan had already revealed his plans to Secretary of the Treasury Chase in early

December, and his friend Blair must have been familiar with them, as was Franklin. However, Lincoln did not force the issue, merely stating that so long as McClellan had some definite date and plan in mind it would be satisfactory. McClellan assured him he had, but made no attempt to see the president in private to reveal the details. And it was Lincoln who said, "I will hold McClellan's horse if he will only bring us success."

To many people in Washington it now appeared as if McClellan might be more interested in the political affairs of the nation rather than its military problems, and this was costing him what little support he had left in the administration and Congress. Although he had ingratiated himself with the Secretary of the Treasury by confiding his plans to him as early as December, Chase was now strongly urging Lincoln to dismiss McClellan. Chase, too, had presidential aspirations, being busily engaged in plans to wrest the Republican nomination from Lincoln in 1864, and he regarded McClellan as a possible threat to these ambitions. And Senators Wade, Trumbull, and Chandler, whom McClellan had used to undermine Scott, were embarrassed by McClellan's inactivity. They had assured their political cohorts that the old general was the only thing holding up a great offensive movement. But, as Radical Republicans and the moving spirits behind the Committee on the Conduct of the War, they were more than embarrassed by McClellan's political activities. They had probably heard rumors of his views as he expressed them in a letter to a friend. "I am fighting to preserve the integrity of the Union," he wrote, "and the power of the Govt—on no other issue. To gain that end we cannot afford to mix up the negro question—it must be incidental and subsidiary." To the Radicals and the vociferous abolitionists this was close to treason, and the uproar against McClellan grew.

"I have a set of men to deal with unscrupulous and false," he now wrote his wife, "if possible they will throw whatever blame there is on my shoulders, and I do not intend to be sacrificed by such people." If he did not move he wanted his wife to know it was not his fault. "I cannot move without more means, and I do not possess the power to control those means. The people think me all-powerful. Never was there a greater mistake." McClellan was discovering that there was no place in the United States, regardless of the emergency, for unlimited military power of the Napoleonic stamp. It was a citizen army, and the people—through the president and the government—would control it and the generals commanding it. It was all in the Constitution: the president and Congress to run the country, the generals to run the Army and fight the wars; but the Constitution made the president the commander in chief to lessen the danger of a military dictatorship ever arising, and also because the American Revolution had demonstrated the inefficiency of Congressional supervision of military leaders. The president would make the final decisions, and the people would hold him responsible for the ultimate results. If the generals wanted 300,000 men and the people, through their president, gave them only 150,000, the job would still have to be done and the generals would have to learn to do the best they could with what they had. McClellan never accepted this fact. "I am thwarted and deceived by these incapables at every turn," he believed.

But time was running out on McClellan. When he failed to inform the president voluntarily of his plans, Lincoln came up with a plan of his own for an overland campaign against the Confederates at Manassas. McClellan objected strongly, substituting his own plan of a movement by water to Urbanna, below Fredericksburg on the lower Rappahannock River, thence overland a short distance to West Point on the York River, and then on to Richmond. Urbanna and West Point would be his major bases, supplied by the Federally controlled water routes. This, said McClellan, would be a brilliant maneuver. He expected to cut off the Confederate force on the lower Virginia peninsula, and at the same time to outmaneuver Johnston at Manassas by getting between his force and Richmond. Of course, all this depended on the Confederates staying exactly where they were and not doing anything about McClellan's movement.

To the legal, logical mind of Lincoln, however, the brilliance of this maneuver was not so evident. He believed that "going down the bay in search of a field, instead of fighting at or near Manassas, was only shifting, and not surmounting, a difficulty." He realized that the Confederates had to be defeated in the field,

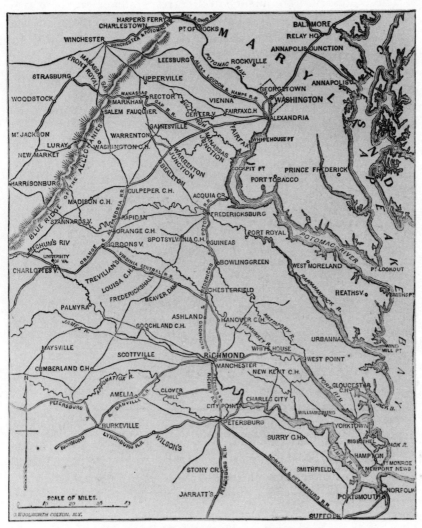

Area of the Peninsula Campaign

and Manassas was only a two days' march away. Also, the president was apprehensive that the move might endanger the safety of Washington, if, as McClellan maintained, Johnston had over 100,000 troops at Manassas.

The discussions, arguments, and correspondence on these two plans dragged on for days. Years later, when the correspondence was released, a New York reporter parodied Lincoln's argument. "If the capital is weakened, it follows very clearly, that it will not be strengthened. My plan is directly the reverse of your plan, so that your plan is immediately opposite to my plan. How can your plan, by differing from my plan, save Washington according to my plan, which is not your plan?"

Finally, however, the president agreed to let McClellan have his way, provided that sufficient troops were left to absolutely insure the safety of Washington. His orders on this were explicit. "Leave such force at Manassas Junction as shall make it entirely certain that the enemy shall not repossess himself of that position and line of communication. Leave Washington entirely secure." The Secretary of War was instructed to set about securing the necessary vessels for transporting the army and its supplies to the new field of operations.

In the face of this new threat, however, Johnston early in March suddenly evacuated his entrenchments at Manassas and retired towards Richmond, thus making McClellan's move by Urbanna impractical. Still rejecting the overland route into Virginia, McClellan now decided to land his army at Fort Monroe and work his way up the peninsula to Richmond, with his supplies coming up the York River.

Then an action took place off the Virginia coast that came close to cancelling all McClellan's plans. When the Federals abandoned Norfolk on the James River early in the war, they had sunk many of their ships, including the 350-ton frigate *Merrimac*. But the Confederates had raised it, and, working furiously, had converted it into an ironclad, renaming it the *Virginia*. On March 8 it steamed out into Hampton Roads and inflicted terrible destruction on the conventional wooden Federal fleet off Fort Monroe. Without control of these waters and the coastline, McClellan's plan was doomed. But the North had also been busy

Fort Monroe

constructing one of the new ironclad gunboats, the *Monitor*, and by March 8 it was ready to be tested. The next day it steamed into Hampton Roads and engaged the *Virginia* in a tremendous duel which proved conclusively that the day of the wooden gunboat was gone. Neither succeeded in sinking the other in this standoff, but the *Virginia* returned to its base in Norfolk to block Federal passage up the James. With the *Monitor* there to protect the Federal fleet against the threat of the Confederate ironclad, however, the York River and the Fort Monroe area were again safe for Federal operation. McClellan could still carry out his plan.

As the transports slowly dropped down the Potomac that chill March day, many in Washington were optimistic that the war would soon be over. How could the South stand up to that magnificent army, so wonderfully trained and splendidly equipped and supplied? To many of the residents of Alexandria, most of whom were Southerners and secessionists at heart, it did not seem possible. The end of the Confederacy seemed near.

The war had not gone well for the South since Manassas. That victory had lulled the people and the Confederate government into a false sense of security. Starting from scratch, all the various government departments, as well as an army, had to be created, organized, and staffed to carry on a war, while at the same time a government had to be set up to pass laws to govern what was hoped would be a new country, the Confederate States of America. With the people of the South not used to hurrying about anything anyway, Manassas seemed to take away all sense of urgency. "We are resting on our oars after the victory at Manassas," wrote J. B. Jones, a clerk in the new War Department. The articulate and observant Mrs. Chesnut, wife of an aide to the Confederate president, put it more succinctly. "That victory did nothing but send us off into a fool's paradise of conceit, and it roused the manhood of the Northern people."

In May, 1861 the Confederate Congress, meeting in Montgomery, Alabama, had voted to remove the Confederate capital to Richmond, Virginia. This decision had been generally welcomed by most Virginians; in fact, they expected it, as the city had been seething with excitement ever since the firing on Fort Sumter. When the news of that event reached Richmond the afternoon of April 12, there was dancing in the streets and bonfires were lit to celebrate the historic event. Cannons were quickly dragged by hand from the state arsenal to Capitol Square to fire a salute. The new Confederate flag was hoisted atop the Capitol building. One observer noted: "One of the remarkable features of the times is that men of all classes and conditions, of all occupations and professions, are of one mind." Five days later Virginia officially seceded from the Union, and former U.S. President John Tyler, a Virginian, wrote: "The contest into which we enter is one full of peril, but there is a spirit abroad in Virginia which cannot be crushed until the life of the last man is trampled out." And the ever observant Russell of the London *Times*, now traveling in the South, wrote: "I am not prepared to say they are right or wrong, but I am convinced that the South can only be forced back by such a conquest as that which laid Poland prostrate at the feet of Russia."

The move to Richmond was logical. Essentially, it was dictated by political and military considerations. The prestige of Virginia, richest and most populous state in the South, was considered nec-

Richmond in 1862

essary for the success of the Confederacy. For political reasons it
was believed that the capital should be near the border states and
the heavy fighting expected there. Second only to New Orleans,
Richmond was the largest city in the Confederacy, having a population of something over 38,000. It was also the center of iron
manufacturing in the South. The Tredegar Iron Works, main
source of cannon supply for the Southern armies, influenced the
choice of Richmond and demanded its defense. During the course
of the war Tredegar made over 1,100 cannons, in addition to
torpedoes, mines, propeller shafts, and other war machinery. It
expanded to include rolling mills, forges, sawmills, and machine
shops. The Richmond Laboratory made over 72 million cartridges, along with grenades, gun carriages, field artillery, and
canteens, while the Richmond Armory had a capacity for manufacturing 6,000 small arms a month. In a South that was basically
agricultural, the protection of these industries was of vital con-
cern.

So if the safety of Washington was the skeleton that haunted
Lincoln's closet, Richmond was the millstone around the neck of
the Confederacy. And yet, once it became the capital it had to be
defended to the last, not only because of its industrial capacity,
but for political and diplomatic reasons. In all probability, if
Richmond had fallen early in the war the Southern effort would

have collapsed. With its capital gone, any hope the Confederacy might have had for European recognition and aid would have gone with it. As the Richmond *Dispatch* stated: "To lose Richmond is to lose Virginia, and to lose Virginia is to lose the key to the Southern Confederacy."

Thus Richmond became the political, military, and manufacturing center of the South, and the very symbol of secession to the North. Situated at the head of the navigable waters of the James River, and within 110 miles of Washington, it was the key to the military planning of both sides; and for four years it remained the primary military objective of the Federal armies in the east.

As the new capital, of course, Richmond underwent a dramatic change. When hundreds of regiments from further south streamed in, the city took on the appearance of a vast military camp. At night the glow from thousands of campfires lit up the sky. People came by the thousands to work in the various government departments and factories. Mrs. Chesnut noted: "There was much music and mustering and marching, much cheering and flying of flags, much firing of guns and all that sort of thing." In their new fancy uniforms the excited recruits posed for portraits,

Richmonders Celebrating Manassas Victory

followed the bands down the springtime streets, waved to the cheering girls, and set about, they thought, getting the war over with in a hurry.

Then came Manassas, and many now believed that the war was as good as over. Men who had signed up for a short term refused to re-enlist, recruiting fell off, and farmers went home to plant crops and did not return, so that by the spring of 1862 the Confederate Army was actually shrinking. Consequently, in order to keep an effective army in the field, the Confederate Congress was forced to resort to a conscription act drafting able-bodied men between eighteen and thirty-five for three years, or the duration if the war ended before that. There were many exemptions, of course, but what aroused the most opposition and bitterness was exempting planters who owned at least twenty slaves. Many violent states' rights men now began to oppose the Confederate government as strongly as they had previously opposed the Federal government. And the small planters and farmers were particularly bitter, calling it now the rich man's war but the poor man's fight. "This war was a volunteer business," noted Mrs. Chesnut. "Tomorrow conscription begins—the last resort."

And the failure of the Confederate forces to follow up the victory at Manassas and march into Washington also aroused bitterness and personal feuds. Although the Richmond *Examiner* could declare, "There is one wild shout of fierce resolve to capture Washington City, at all and every human hazard," the truth was that the Southern army was almost as disorganized by the victory as the Northern army was by the defeat. Like the Northern army, it was mainly an army of raw recruits, ill trained, poorly equipped, and lacking discipline, led by inexperienced officers. Supplies and transportation were lacking, and the two generals, Beauregard and Johnston, could not agree on any plan of action. When Jefferson Davis, president of the Confederacy, came on the field the night of the battle, Johnston insisted his men were too exhausted and wagons were lacking, and Beauregard stated the entrenchments around Washington were too formidable. When Davis suggested several different methods of attacking the city, his generals expressed their inability to cross the Potomac. Like Lincoln, Davis was having trouble with his generals. Also, his habit of appearing on the field of battle in person and attempting to give tactical orders did nothing to increase his popularity.

Davis, like Lincoln, considered himself responsible to the people for the overall strategy of the war, as implied in the title commander in chief. The ultimate responsibility for decisions was his, but being a graduate of West Point, a colonel in the Mexican War, and a former Secretary of War of the United States, he considered himself an expert on tactics also, and a field command was what his heart desired, not the presidency.

Jefferson Davis was born in Kentucky a year earlier than Lincoln in 1808. He was named after a great president, Jefferson, a Virginian who believed that a little rebellion once in a while was a good thing. While Lincoln moved at an early age to Indiana and then Illinois, Davis was taken as a baby into the Deep South, Louisiana and Mississippi, where he grew up in the new cotton-planter aristocracy. When Lincoln lost his first love before they could be married, he grew moody and melancholy. When Davis lost his first bride three months after the wedding, he retreated into a world of books and theories for several years, and grew moody and sensitive to criticism. Like Lincoln again, Davis lost a little boy in the Confederate White House during the war.

Although a strong believer in the right of secession and slavery, he was not regarded as a radical secessionist, despite the fact that in 1860 he joined with the arch radicals to split the Democratic Party into Northern and Southern factions, thus assuring Republican Lincoln's election. Davis owed his election primarily to his military experience and his moderate political views.

A cold, phlegmatic type of person, he was nevertheless a handsome, impressive-looking man, even though blind in one eye and constantly ill with dyspepsia and nervous attacks. His haughty manner and icy formality, however, tended to alienate people and made it impossible for him to manage and use the best in them, as Lincoln did so successfully. His second wife wrote of him, "If anyone differs with Mr. Davis, he resents it and ascribes the difference to the perversity of his opponent."

At Manassas, however, he did not overrule his generals, although from then on he carried on a feud with Johnston and

Beauregard that lasted throughout the war. Instead, he returned to Richmond determined "to employ all the power of my office to increase the strength of the army." Unfortunately, however, because of the false sense of security engendered by the events at Manassas, he was forced by spring of 1862 to request the passage of the Conscription Act in order to achieve his objective.

But even with the draft and the manpower it would raise, Davis's troubles were just beginning. As the warm, pleasant April days came with the large Federal army landing at Fort Monroe, there were many who doubted the ability of the Confederate government and army to defend Richmond, or even the wisdom of attempting it. It was suspected, for example, that General Johnston favored making a stand farther south or in the west, rather than tackle the difficult task of defending the city. And the war in the west was going poorly for the Confederacy. With the fall of Forts Henry and Donelson in Tennessee, Federal forces had gained control of the Cumberland and Tennessee rivers and were now moving down the Mississippi. New Orleans, the South's most valuable seaport, had fallen under naval attack, and when the two Union forces met on the Mississippi the Confederacy would be cut in two and the great supply bin of Texas would be lost.

At one meeting called by Davis to consider the situation, the participants were suddenly startled when General Robert E. Lee, Davis's military advisor, burst out with "Richmond must not be given up. It shall not be given up." Coming from a normally calm, soft-spoken man, this emotional outburst surprised not only those who did not know Lee well, but also Davis, who did and who had personally selected him as his advisor.

It was not surprising that most of the high-ranking officials of the Confederate government did not know Lee well at this time. His only field command in the war had been a small affair in western Virginia, which, unfortunately, had ended in a Confederate retreat. In rough, mountainous country he had planned a surprise attack at Cheat Mountain, which was to be the signal for a simultaneous attack on Valley River. But because of a heavy storm, the exhaustion of the poorly trained troops, and the inexperience of the officers, the attack at Cheat Mountain never took place, the plan was discovered by the Federals, and Lee was forced to withdraw. For this he was abused by the press, earning the sobriquet "Evacuating Lee," and even some of his friends began to think he had been overrated. In an address after the war Davis stated: "He came back, carrying the heavy weight of defeat, and unappreciated by the people whom he served, for they could not know, as I knew, that, if his plans and orders had been carried out, the result would have been victory rather than retreat." Yet it was characteristic of the man that he would not alibi or attempt to place the blame for the failure elsewhere. He reported to the governor of Virginia: "The attack to come off from the east side failed from the difficulties in the way; the opportunity was lost, and our plan discovered. It is a grievous disappointment to me, I assure you." And to his wife he confessed, "I can not tell you my regret and mortification at the untoward events that caused the failure of the plan."

A tall, dignified, handsome man, Lee was born in Virginia in 1807, the son of Henry "Light-Horse Harry" Lee of Revolutionary War fame. Graduating from the Military Academy at West Point in 1829, he served as a colonel in the Mexican War under General Scott, a command which earned him a brilliant reputation. From 1852 to 1853 he was superintendent of the Military Academy, and later accepted an assignment with the cavalry in Texas, a post from which he was recalled on the outbreak of war. If he was not well known to the political officials of the Confederacy, he was to the professional military people on both sides, particularly Scott. Acting on Scott's advice, President Lincoln in April, 1861 offered Lee the command of the United States Army in the field, which he declined, stating "that though opposed to secession and deprecating war, I could take no part in an invasion of the Southern States." A few days later, after much mental anguish, he resigned his commission, telling General Scott of "the struggle it has cost me to separate myself from a service to which I have devoted the best years of my life, and all the ability I possessed. . . . Save in the defense of my native State, I never desire again to draw my sword."

Lee had two priceless gifts for a military career, patience with the weaknesses of men and unforeseen circumstances, and an unusual ability to understand and lead people. Always reticent, neither jealous nor unduly ambitious, he was extremely patriotic with a strong sense of loyalty, particularly to his family and state. To him duty was the "sublimest word in the language." He strongly opposed secession and hated slavery. "Secession is nothing but revolution," he declared. "In this enlightened age, there are few I believe, but what will acknowledge, that slavery as an institution is a moral and political evil in any country." When Virginia seceded, however, he could not answer, nor could anyone else to his satisfaction, his question, "But how can I draw my sword against Virginia?" To him there was no answer. "It is the principle I contend for," he wrote, "not individual or private benefit."

Walt Whitman the poet called it "a strange, sad war," and strange it most assuredly was. Lee, who hated slavery and secession, worked in harmony with Davis, who supported both, to destroy the Union. McClellan, who had no desire to abolish slavery, refused to work with Lincoln, who opposed slavery and secession, and desired only to preserve the Union.

A few days after Lee resigned his commission the governor appointed him to the command of all Virginia's forces in the field, but as soon as Davis reached Richmond he immediately selected Lee as his personal military advisor. Under the circumstances, then, Lee's unusual show of emotion regarding the defense of Richmond was understandable, even if not characteristic, and his influence prevailed. Davis decided to order Johnston's army to join the small force under General John B. Magruder then stationed in the vicinity of Yorktown on the lower peninsula. The Confederate government was now committed to the defense of Richmond at all costs.

Seven Pines:
The Army of the Potomac
Proves Its Mettle

By the first week in April the Army of the Potomac had landed on the Virginia peninsula, much to the relief of the men, most of whom had been violently seasick during the passage. It was a quiet land they came to, this peninsula between the York and the James rivers, unspectacular but pleasing and colorful to the eye. A gently rolling country of soft ridges and quiet woods that stretched eighty miles east of Richmond to Hampton Roads and the Atlantic. Basically a flat plain, it was intersected by hundreds of small creeks, gullies, and swamps, most of which fed into or bordered on the marshy Chickahominy River as it meandered diagonally across the peninsula in a southeasterly direction to where it emptied into the James just west of Williamsburg. Many times these creeks ended in small but sharp ravines where the thick honeysuckle and tanglefoot underbrush ranged far and

40

Federal Supply Base at Fort Monroe

wide in wild abandon. The whole plain was interlaced with narrow dirt roads, some of which seemed to have a purpose and went
someplace, but many of them went nowhere, suddenly disappearing in the dark woods and swamps or ending up at a farmhouse
or church, miles from anywhere. These roads were not planned
or built in the usual sense; they just materialized from local usage
for local convenience. Even the natives were not familiar with all
of them, and they could get lost as quickly and easily as the
stranger.

There were still some of the traditional southern plantation
houses along the rivers, beautiful reminders of a day and way of
life that was gone from this section of the Old Dominion. These
had mostly been tobacco plantations, all close to the rivers for
easy transportation of the valuable yellow weed. But this single-
crop system had exhausted most of the soil, and the land was
gradually changing over to the diversified crops of general farm-
ing, with a ready market in the growing city of Richmond. The
area was sparsely populated, though, with farms few and far between and almost three-quarters of the land in timber.

Now a great Federal army lay sprawled to the north and east of Richmond, with its supply line stretching all the way down the peninsula. The men and boys who made up this army, almost half of whom were farmers when peace was on the land, appreciated the rich soil and abundant orchards, but deplored the wastefulness that left half the land uncultivated. They also hated the constant rains that loosened the topsoil, where it was not nailed down with roots, and churned it into a red clayish mud that stuck like glue. They could joke about it—"Virginia used to be in the Union; now it's in the mud"—but they would never forget it. A veteran of the Thirteenth Massachusetts Volunteers remembered that "the amount of muscular energy required to lift your feet with ten pounds or more of mud clinging to each foot, can hardly be appreciated except by persons who have a knowledge of the 'sacred soil' of Virginia."

The mud, however, was the least of General McClellan's worries. Upon his arrival he was informed that the Confederates were drawn up behind a line of entrenchments from Yorktown across to the Warwick River, "garrisoned by not less than 15,000 troops under command of General John B. Magruder." Actually, Magruder probably had less than 10,000 troops at the time. Optimistically McClellan informed his wife, "I hope to get possession of Yorktown day after tomorrow." Then he received a message informing him that one corps of about 30,000 men under McDowell's command had been detained for the defense of Washington and would not join him in the coming campaign. "It is the most infamous thing that history has recorded," he angrily informed his wife. This still left him with over 100,000 men, the largest army ever commanded by one man in the history of the Western Hemisphere, but he immediately wired the Secretary of War that it would now be "necessary to resort to the use of heavy guns and some siege operations before we assault," and accused the administration of not supporting him. "It seems clear that I shall have the whole force of the enemy on my hands—probably not less than 100,000 men, and possibly more."

In a long answering letter the patient Lincoln tried to explain the facts of life to McClellan. He told him politely that his accusations about not being supported, "while they do not offend me, do pain me very much." Then he stated emphatically: "My explicit order that Washington should, by the judgement of all the commanders of army corps, be left entirely secure, had been neglected. It was precisely this that drove me to detain McDowell." He went on to warn McClellan that the enemy would gain by delay, and earnestly advised that it was "indispensable to you that you strike a blow. I am powerless to help this. . . . The country will not fail to note, is now noting, that the present hesitation to move upon an entrenched enemy is but the story of Manassas repeated." Then assuring McClellan that he would do all in his power to help him, he ended with the stern admonition: "But you must act."

All of this, of course, was lost on McClellan. He did not regard his commander in chief's words as orders or even advice, merely arrogant interference in an attempt to block his success and thus ruin him politically. "History will present a sad record of these traitors," he wrote, "who were willing to sacrifice the country and its army for personal spite and personal aims." And despite the almost desperate plea by the president for immediate action, McClellan had no intention of abandoning his siege operations in favor of an assault. As he explained to his wife, he would attack Yorktown only when he could do it successfully by siege with heavy guns. "But I don't intend to hurry it; I cannot afford to fail. I may have the opportunity of carrying the place next week, or may be delayed a couple of weeks." It didn't seem to matter, one way or another, to McClellan. He was happy in the belief that he was "avoiding the fault of the Allies at Sebastopol, and quietly preparing the way for great success."

That, of course, was what he told his wife, which was probably the truth. Officially, however, his reason for not acting was his charge that the government was not sustaining him, by which he meant he did not have enough men. On April 7 he wrote Secretary of War Stanton that he had only "about 85,000 men for duty, from which a large force must be taken for guards, scouts, etc." His plan, he said, was to send a separate force to take Gloucester Point, across the York River from Yorktown, thus enabling the gunboats to ascend the river and bypass the fortifications. But he could not carry out this plan, he claimed, because the government would not support him properly. "My present strength will not admit of a detachment sufficient for this purpose without materially impairing the efficiency of this column."

This not only pained Lincoln, it also confused him. "There is a curious mystery about the number of troops now with you," he wrote April 9. "When I telegraphed you on the 6th, saying you had over a hundred thousand with you, I had just obtained from the Secretary of War a statement, taken, as he said, from your own returns, making 108,000 then with you and en route to you. You now say you will have but 85,000 when all en route to you shall have reached you. How can this discrepancy of 23,000 be accounted for?"

Writing his memoirs after the war in 1882, McClellan claimed that the figure of 108,000 given the president was wrong, and charged Stanton with deliberately using the total figure of those present and absent to make him look bad. McClellan claimed that his figure of 85,000, which showed only the actual number present for duty, was the one that should have been used. The fact remains, however, that a report signed by McClellan himself on April 13 showed that the Army of the Potomac had 100,970 present for duty, 4,265 on special detail, and 12,486 absent, for a grand total of 117,721.

Regardless of whether or not he intended to make the move on Gloucester Point, McClellan insisted he could not make it without Franklin's division of McDowell's corps, about 12,000 men. "Franklin and his division are indispensable to me," he telegraphed Stanton on April 10. The fact that Franklin was a personal friend of his might have had something to do with it also. The worried Lincoln decided to give him what he wanted, however, in the fond hope that it just might produce results. With the addition of Franklin's division, McClellan now had a total of 130,000 men, which he organized into five corps, commanded by Generals E. V. Sumner, S. P. Heintzelman, Erasmus D. Keyes, Fitz John Porter, and William B. Franklin. "I am delighted with Franklin's orders," he telegraphed, "and beg to thank you. I shall make the movement I alluded to as soon as possible after he arrives."

Needless to say, the movement was never made. A week later he was begging Stanton: "Give me McCall's division and I will undertake a movement on West Point which will shake them out of Yorktown." That had always been his plan, he insisted, but he expected to have nearly 150,000 troops to carry it out. Now, with only 130,000 he could not do it unless he had McCall's division of McDowell's corps. Otherwise, "I must not be blamed if success is delayed." Two days earlier though, he had sent the president a confidential dispatch. "After all that I have heard of things which have occurred since I left Washington and before, I would prefer that General McDowell should not again be assigned to duty with me." The same day he wrote his wife, "No general ever labored under greater disadvantages, but I will carry it through in spite of everything."

And so the days passed, rainy days, with McClellan slowly dragging his siege guns through the mud, digging gigantic entrenchments for them, until he had 114 heavy guns and mortars in position ready to open fire on Yorktown. Then, on May 4, the Confederates wisely withdrew up the peninsula towards Richmond. This, however, forced them to abandon Norfolk, the base of the Confederate ironclad *Merrimac*, the dreadnought which had effectively blocked the James to the Federals and forced them to keep the *Monitor* in Hampton Roads. With its base gone, the crew of the *Merrimac* blew it up on the advice of river pilots that it could not navigate the treacherous channel up the James.

The South had gained by McClellan's hesitation, however. As Lincoln had warned him, his delay had enabled the Confederates to build up their forces. When McClellan first landed on the peninsula, Magruder had less than 10,000 troops. But when McClellan resorted to siege tactics instead of assaulting, and the Confederate government was convinced that the landing was not just a feint, Johnston was immediately ordered down the peninsula to join Magruder, so that when he withdrew from Yorktown he had in the neighborhood of 60,000 men, with reinforcements still coming into Richmond from the Deep South.

McClellan sent a column to pursue the fleeing Rebels, but it was stopped with a rearguard action at Williamsburg. Hampered by the deep mud and heavy rains, McClellan did not attempt any further pursuit overland. Instead, on May 6 he sent Franklin's division up the York River by transport to take and hold West Point. The Pamunkey River joined the York at West Point, and the Richmond & York River Railroad connected it directly with Richmond. McClellan had always believed that West Point was the key to the whole region because of the railroad and its connection with the navigable river, and now believed erroneously that that was where Johnston was heading.

Johnston, however, was only interested in the safety of his wagon train, and did not attempt to hold the terminus at West Point, but he did attack Franklin on May 7 under the impression that McClellan was attempting to cut his train off from Richmond. The attack was repulsed, but the train continued on in safety as Franklin's orders were simply to hold until reinforcements arrived. This engagement was known as the Battle of West Point or Eltham's Landing.

In the meantime, McClellan gradually got the great ponderous machine that was the Army of the Potomac in motion up the peninsula toward West Point. But progress was slow. The wettest spring in anyone's memory was at hand. It rained and kept raining, day after dreary day. Dirt roads turned into bottomless mud; creeks and gullies became swift-flowing streams; fields were swamps. At the end of each long, weary day the rain-soaked soldier went into bivouac, tired, muddy, and foot-sore. He built his little campfire, fried his hardtack and pork, brewed his coffee, and fell asleep, as one veteran recalled, "with feet wet, boots for a pillow, and the mud oozing up around our rubber blankets."

Miles and miles of roads, axle-deep in muck, had to be corduroyed to support the supply wagons and field artillery. General Van Vliet, McClellan's quartermaster, reported disgustedly that he had "never seen worse roads in any part of the country. Teams cannot haul over half a load, and often empty wagons are stalled." And it required over 500 tons of forage and subsistence daily to supply and feed the men and animals in the field and on the march.

Washington, of course, was bitterly disappointed that McClellan had let Johnston escape, and was growing impatient at the slow progress being made towards Richmond. Lincoln remarked bitterly to his secretary that, "McClellan seemed to think, in defiance of Scripture, that heaven sent its rain only on the just and not on the unjust." But there was little that McClellan could do about it. Johnston had a head start, and with the execrable condition of the roads and the monsoon weather it was impossible to overtake him. Also he was not burdened with all the heavy artillery and supplies that the Union Army carried, and he was retreating towards his base of supply, not away from it.

If McClellan had only refrained from making rash promises and bombastic statements, his relations with Washington could have been much smoother. Flushed with the victory of Yorktown, he immediately bombarded Lincoln and Stanton with Napoleonic declarations. "No time shall be lost. I shall push the enemy to the wall. . . . The success is brilliant. . . . There shall be no delay in following up the rebels." This optimistic mood lasted less than three days; then it became the same old refrain. He couldn't move because of the weather, the roads, lack of wagons, shortage of transports, the bridges. He had also discovered that the Rebels had a force of 120,000 in front of Franklin, so again he wanted "all the re-enforcements that can be given me," although he had not as yet fought a battle. To nonmilitary minds, of course, this didn't make sense. Why, if the Confederates were superior in numbers, had they abandoned Yorktown without a fight? McClellan did not bother to explain.

As soon as word was received that Norfolk was abandoned and the *Merrimac* destroyed, McClellan wired Stanton: "I would now most earnestly urge that our gunboats and the iron-clad boats be sent as far as possible up the James River without delay. This will enable me to make our movements much more decisive." He had previously assured the War Department that the "Navy will receive prompt support wherever and whenever required." Gideon Welles, Secretary of the Navy, immediately issued instructions to Flag Officer Goldsborough at Hampton Roads: "Push all the boats you can spare up James River even to Richmond." Five Union gunboats, including the famous *Monitor*, started up the James under Commander John Rogers aboard the *Galena.* By May 15 they reached Drewry's Bluff, just seven miles below Richmond. Here, at a sharp bend, the Confederates had effectively obstructed the river and erected powerful batteries on the ninety-foot bluff. At seven o'clock that morning the gunboats opened fire. The battle raged for four hours while the fate of Richmond, and quite possibly the Confederacy, hung in the balance. Finally, however, the accurate fire of the heavy guns on the bluff, combined with effective sharpshooting along the riverbanks, proved too much for the gunboats and the Federal fleet retreated back down the river. A Confederate officer observed: "Had Commander Rogers been supported by a few brigades, landed at City Point or above on the south side, Richmond would have been evacuated."

Although the Navy requested "a cooperating land force" to help the gunboats pass Drewry's Bluff and take Richmond, McClellan, despite his earlier promise of cooperation, wired the War Department: "Am not yet ready to cooperate with them." He neglected to mention when he would be ready.

At this point, it appears that McClellan was afraid the Navy would get the credit for the capture of Richmond if the gunboats succeeded in reaching the city. There had always been a doubt in his mind, and there still was, that the Rebels would offer serious resistance. He believed the evacuation of Norfolk and the destruction of the *Merrimac* signified the Rebels' intention to abandon Richmond if seriously threatened. His heavy siege guns would be threat enough, he believed, to force evacuation. All he needed was time and the fame and glory would be his.

Many citizens of Richmond shared McClellan's conviction that the Southern capital was impossible to defend. That morning of May 15 near panic swept the city. War clerk Jones noted, "If the enemy pass the obstructions, the city will be, it is true, very much at their mercy." The Treasury Department loaded the gold and silver bullion on railroad cars, ready to roll. Hundreds fled the city, including President Davis's family. The tide seemed to be running out for the Confederacy. "Is there no turning point in this long lane of downward progress," Jones wondered sadly.

Then, as if in answer to his question, came the news: the Federal fleet was repulsed and retreating down the river. The people breathed freely again. The crisis was past; the turning point had been reached at last. "The panic here has subsided," Davis could write to his wife, "and with increasing confidence there has arisen a desire to see the city destroyed rather than surrender."

But Johnston was still retreating and the president was worried. On May 17 he wrote to the general, "To you it is needless to say that the defense must be made outside the city." Two days later, to Davis's consternation, Johnston's forces were practically in the suburbs, and the Richmond newspapers criticized both Johnston and Davis bitterly. Johnston then tried to explain to Lee why he could not act. "We are engaged in a species of warfare at which we can never win. It is plain that Gen. McClellan will adhere to the system adapted by him last summer, and depend for success upon artillery and engineering. We can compete with him in neither." This was true, but only if Johnston intended to fight McClellan's kind of battle. Neither Davis nor Lee could get any definite commitment from Johnston as to what he did intend to do, but both became convinced that he wanted to retreat west or south rather than attempt the defense of Richmond. It was now evident that Davis was losing confidence in his field commander, and Johnston bitterly resented the president's interference in military matters. Under the patient prodding of Lee, however, who could do more with him than Davis could, Johnston finally agreed to plan an attack when the right opportunity presented itself.

The news of the opening of the James, despite the repulse of May 15, was received with joy in Washington, and everyone now hoped that an immediate attack could be made on Richmond. But McClellan made no motion to show that he intended to take advantage of the situation. Instead, he pushed on up the York past West Point, and then up the Pamunkey River. At the area known as White House, where the railroad crossed the Pamunkey on its way to West Point, he was establishing a gigantic supply base. Over 400 transports were busily shuttling up and down the rivers laden with stores, supplies, and equipment. On McClellan's request, five steam locomotives and eighty cars were shipped from Alexandria to get the railroad started.

Lincoln had hoped, as he informed McClellan, "that the opening of James River . . . with an open road to Richmond, or to you, had effected something in that direction." If McClellan ever had any plans to attack Richmond along the line of the James, now was the time to reveal them. But all the president got from his general was a long telegram complaining that he had only 80,000 troops to use against Richmond and that he desperately needed reinforcements as the enemy had at least twice as many men as he had. And he was even willing to take McDowell now, which apparently was supposed to prove to the president how critical his situation really was. Of course, it was always "possible that Richmond may be abandoned without a serious struggle," but even so, "if more troops than I now have should prove unnecessary for purposes of military occupation, our greatest display of imposing force in the capital of the rebel government will have the best moral effect." In other words, fight or no fight, for history's sake at least, McClellan simply had to have a larger army. To his wife he complained, "My government, alas!, is not giving me any aid. . . ."

To Lincoln and everyone else in the government, McClellan's arithmetic was confusing, to say the least. Before he received Franklin's division he had insisted that he had only 85,000 effectives. Now, after Franklin's arrival, he was down to 80,000. Not only had Franklin's 12,000 men disappeared, but another 5,000 along with them. It was little wonder the president remarked disgustedly that sending troops to McClellan was like shoveling fleas across a barnyard: half of them never got there. The truth was, McClellan's own report for May 20 showed a total force of 128,000, with 102,000 present and equipped for combat. Nevertheless, Lincoln decided to gamble to some extent with the safety of Washington, and agreed to let McClellan have McDowell's corps of about 35,000 men, with the provision that they must proceed overland, not by water as McClellan requested, thus always keeping themselves between Richmond and Washington. McClellan was ordered to cooperate by keeping his right wing north of Richmond to establish communication with McDowell when he arrived.

Years later, an embittered ex-soldier and unsuccessful presidential candidate, McClellan stated in his memoirs that this order caused the failure of the whole campaign by forcing him to put his right wing north of Richmond, thus keeping his army split by the Chickahominy River and forcing him to use the York rather than the James. Some historians and apologists for Mc-Clellan accept this thesis without question and place the blame for failure on Lincoln and Washington for interference. The fact is, however, there is not one shred of evidence to support this theory.

From the very beginning, McClellan planned to use the York River as his avenue of approach and line of supply. Even his first plan, to proceed by way of Urbanna, had as its immediate objective the possession of West Point on the York, which he believed to be "the key of that region." When the Urbanna approach became impractical with the Confederate withdrawal from Manassas, McClellan then substituted the move by way of Fort Monroe and up the peninsula, but with West Point still the objective. Only in the event that this plan should fail did he even suggest a James River move, and then he merely stated in general terms that they could cross the James and throw the army in the rear of Richmond. It was not until he wrote his official report, when the campaign was over, that McClellan suggested the James River approach and claimed Washington's interference prevented it.

The order for McDowell to join the Army of the Potomac was sent May 18. It must be remembered that McClellan had possession of West Point May 7, Norfolk fell three days later, and the next day the *Merrimac* was scuttled. The James was open either as an avenue of approach or supply line or both. McClellan then requested the Navy to send the gunboats up the James, but only to protect his flank apparently, as he made no attempt to use the river. When, on May 15, the Federal fleet was stopped at Drewry's Bluff, McClellan refused to cooperate to reduce the fortifications. "Circumstances," he declared vaguely, "must determine the propriety of a land attack," although he admitted at the same time that before any attack on Richmond from the James could be made these fortifications would have to be reduced. Earlier, on May 10, he had informed Washington that he *could* change his line "to the James River and dispense with the railroad," if Norfolk was captured and the *Merrimac* destroyed, but obviously he had no intention of doing so, because on May 14 he requested "that the rolling stock and material for repairs of West Point and Richmond railway be shipped to West Point at once."

Writing in 1882, McClellan stated that the president's order "forced" him to establish his base on the Pamunkey, whereas, in fact, he had already set up his supply depots at White House and West Point by May 15. It is true that McClellan requested Mc-Dowell be sent by water, but this had nothing to do with McClellan keeping his right wing where it already was, northeast of Richmond, because if McDowell came by water he had to come up the York; the Army of the Potomac was not on the James and had no plans to move there. All McClellan was worried about, as he complained in a long telegram to the president, was that he would not be able to exercise full control over McDowell under the president's orders. As far as McClellan's strategical position and plans were concerned, it made no difference whether Mc-Dowell came by water or land.

The point is, McClellan was guilty of a tactical blunder and a logistical miscalculation. With his bases at White House and West Point, his army had to straddle the Chickahominy River in any attack on Richmond, and McClellan grossly underestimated the obstacle that river could be in bad weather. On the other hand, he overestimated the logistical value of the railroad from West Point to Richmond. It was a single track line and sections were continually being washed away by the constant rains. General Van Vliet reported that although the railroad was of some help, the greater part of the army was not on it, so "most of our supplies are obliged to be transported by wagon."

As it developed, McClellan did not have McDowell for long. The president telegraphed him May 24 that because of the actions of Confederate General "Stonewall" Jackson in the Shenandoah Valley, he was compelled to suspend McDowell's order to join him. McClellan replied that he had not expected McDowell to reach him in time for the attack on Richmond anyway, so his

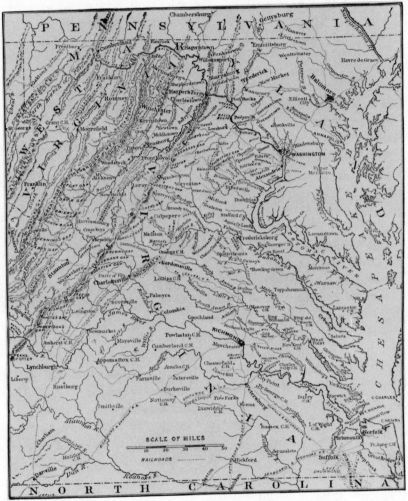

Area of the Virginia Campaigns

plans were not changed. "Delays on my part will be dangerous," he informed the already alarmed president.

Believing that the safety of Washington was again endangered, Lincoln and his cabinet felt that Rebel reinforcements must have been sent into the Valley; so it seemed logical to them that Mc-Clellan should now either put pressure on Richmond or return to the defense of the capital. The next day Lincoln wired: "I think the time is near when you must either attack Richmond or give up the job and come to the defense of Washington."

By this time McClellan had his army established on a front partly encircling Richmond on the north and east, and less than six miles from the city. Three corps, the II, V, and VI, under Sumner, Porter, and Franklin, lined the north bank of the Chickahominy, while the III and IV corps, commanded by Heintzelman and Keyes, were south of the river, astride the York River Railroad and the roads down the peninsula. But he had only one bridge connecting these two wings. Believing, however, that he needed only two additional bridges, he informed the president that "the time is very near when I shall attack Richmond." The same day he wrote his wife, "Heaven save a country governed by such counsels."

But McClellan was not to get his bridges that easy. On May 30 a violent rainstorm lashed the peninsula, continuing into the night. The Chickahominy, normally a slow, sluggish stream, became a raging torrent, rising three to four feet above normal. The low, swampy bottomlands, which bordered it on either side, varying from half a mile to a mile in width and fringed with a dense growth of trees, became completely impassable. Corduroyed roads, on which so much precious time and energy had been expended, disappeared in the mud. Bridges became dangerous for infantry and suicidal for artillery, as the swollen river ripped and tore at the foundations, threatening all with destruction. It was a perfect time for an attack on the two corps south of the river, where, under the circumstances, it would be almost impossible to reinforce them.

Johnston saw the opportunity and acted. Early the next morning in the heavy rain he hurled twenty-three of his twenty-seven brigades at the III and IV Corps south of the river in the area

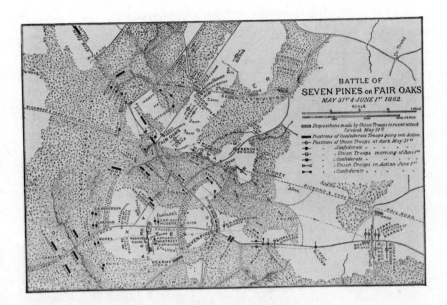

Battle of Seven Pines

known as Seven Pines or Fair Oaks. Surprised by the sudden, vicious assault, the Federals were pushed back towards the river until their position became precarious. But then the attack started to falter. Directed by vague, verbal orders, instead of explicit written ones, whole brigades got lost, took the wrong roads, and generally got in each other's way. Nine of the attacking brigades never really got into the fight at all. Despite these mistakes, however, only the timely arrival of old General Sumner, who heroically led two divisions of his corps across the tottering Grapevine Bridge against the advice of his engineers, prevented a costly disaster. Late in the day Johnston was seriously wounded and the command fell to General G. W. Smith, but the fighting ceased with darkness.

Early next morning, June 1, Smith renewed the attack, but the reinforced Federals pushed him back and regained the lost ground, causing Smith to withdraw. Instead of following up this advantage, McClellan now put the men to work digging a new line of entrenchments in case of another attack, and offering, as he stated, "a safe retreat in the event of disaster." It was charac-

Sumner's Troops Crossing Grapevine Bridge at Seven Pines

teristic of McClellan that he was always prepared for disaster and retreat, but seldom seemed to know what to do with a victory.

Although the battle itself was indecisive, the casualties were heavy on both sides. The Confederates lost about 6,000 in killed, wounded, and missing; the Federals about 5,000. Despite this loss, however, McClellan still did not want to change his base of operations. Instead, he wanted more and better bridges built across the Chickahominy, eleven in all; and he moved the bulk of his army to the south side, leaving only one corps to protect his supply line and bases at White House and West Point. Again, in his official report of the campaign, he charges that because Mc-dowell's orders were only suspended, not revoked, he was "forced" to keep one corps north of the Chickahominy. This was arrant nonsense. As long as his bases were on the Pamunkey and the York rivers, he would have to keep at least one corps north of the Chickahominy to protect them and his supply line, and Mc-Clellan evidenced no desire to change them, even though, from a logistical standpoint, his situation was absurd. He was supplying four-fifths of his army across the treacherous Chickahominy, whereas, if he changed his base of operations to the James he would have to supply only one-fifth across the river. Also, tactically, his position was faulty and dangerous. As was mentioned earlier, any attack on Richmond based on the York would have to straddle the Chickahominy. But based on the James, McClellan's left flank would be protected by the Federal gunboats on the river, and his right flank, if he withdrew his whole force south of the Chickahominy and destroyed the bridges, would be guarded to a great extent by that river. If and when McDowell came, one corps could be extended to meet him north of Richmond, because then McClellan would not need the river to protect his right flank.

McClellan, of course, regarded the battle of Seven Pines as a great victory, which in a sense it was, as the attack had been repulsed successfully and it proved that the Army of the Potomac was a well-trained, disciplined army, an army willing and ready to fight, with little chance of another Manassas. Seven Pines gave the troops the self-confidence they so desperately needed. And once again McClellan was full of confidence. "I only wait for the river to fall to cross with the rest of the force and make a general attack . . . the morale of my troops is now such that I can venture much, and do not fear for the odds against me." This frame of mind changed again in a few days, however; he did not have enough troops to protect his right and rear—the enemy had over 180,000 men. To replace the casualties suffered at Seven Pines, the president had already given McClellan the troops previously under General John Wool in and about Norfolk and Fort Monroe, about 14,000, to use for housekeeping details and guard duty. Now McCall's division of McDowell's corps, about 12,000 strong, was being shipped to the peninsula by transport. With the troops he already had, minus any casualties, these reinforcements would give McClellan a total force of 149,000, which should have enabled him to carry out any plan he desired. According to his own statement he had expected to have about 150,000 at the start of the campaign; now he had them even without McDowell.

"I shall be in perfect readiness to move forward and take Richmond the moment McCall reaches here and the ground will admit the passage of artillery," McClellan informed his government. McCall arrived June 13, but by then of course McClellan had changed his mind again. Now he wanted a substantial part of General Halleck's army in Mississippi which had recently captured Corinth. Of course, they might not arrive in time to take part in the attack on Richmond, but the "moral effect would be great." It is not surprising that Lincoln exclaimed in frustration and despair, "If I gave General McClellan all the troops he wanted they would not have room to lie down. They would have to sleep standing up."

The weather, of course, was something no one could do anything about. The first week in June it rained constantly while the men struggled waist-deep in water to repair and build the bridges, and knee-deep in mud to corduroy the approaches to them. As one bedraggled soldier wrote: "It would have pleased us much to have seen those 'On-to-Richmond' people put over a 5 mile course in the Virginia mud, loaded with a 40-pound knapsack, 60 rounds of cartridges, and haversacks filled with 4 days rations."

But as the rain gradually diminished and the roads started to dry out under the burning Virginia sun, Washington and the rest of the North could not understand McClellan's failure to move. The trouble was, when McClellan said he was waiting for the roads to admit the passage of artillery, he did not mean light field pieces, he meant his heavy siege guns. His only plan of attack was to advance gradually by regular approaches, that is, advance a half-mile or so, then shell the enemy out of position and advance a little again, until eventually he had them pushed into Richmond and he could conduct a regular siege. As he explained to his wife: "I shall make the first battle mainly an artillery combat . . . I will push them in upon Richmond and behind their works; then I will bring up my heavy guns, shell the city, and carry it by assault."

The pressure on Lincoln, meanwhile, was becoming almost unbearable. More important than the rantings of the politicians, newspapers, and abolitionists, was the fact that with the fall of

Corinth McClellan and the peninsula became the center of worldwide interest. On June 20 the British Parliament was to vote on a resolution for intervention on the side of the South in the American Civil War. France had an army in Mexico and was preparing to send its navy with 25,000 reinforcements. If McClellan failed to take Richmond, France expected the United States to collapse and the British to vote for intervention, in which case she wanted to be prepared to claim her share of the spoils, and Spain would follow England and France.

Lincoln's darkest hour seemed to be at hand. Everything depended on McClellan, and the president was rapidly losing confidence in his general. When he humbly suggested that he could "better dispose of things if I could know about what day you can attack Richmond," McClellan's answer bordered on insolence. He would attack when Providence permitted, when the weather changed, when the roads improved, and when he had completed some necessary details. In the meantime, the president would be glad to know the defensive works were almost completed, and that McClellan would be glad to state his views on the state of affairs throughout the country. All this was fine, of course, except that the president and the country had the general impression that McClellan was supposed to be marching on Richmond, not digging defensive positions, and it appeared to Lincoln that if McClellan didn't do something soon there probably wouldn't be a country to worry about anyway.

If Lincoln was losing confidence in his general, the men in the army were not. To them he was still known affectionately as "Little Mac." They had full confidence in him and in themselves, and Seven Pines had shown they would never run away from a fight again. So, as the rain ceased and the hot June sun baked down, they went swimming, fished in the quiet pools of the Chickahominy, and listened to the croaking bullfrogs in the swamps and the call of the bobwhites in the deep woods. They read and wrote letters, played checkers and chess, or the old army game on a blanket, using yellow corn kernels for chips. When they became bored, they watched the quartermaster troops butchering beef, or other regiments at dress parade or bayonet drill, listened to the many fine regimental bands, or visited back and forth with friends in other outfits. On pay days, or other days if they were lucky at cards, they could visit the sutlers and pick up such things as canned peaches, canned beef and ham, sardines, condensed milk, wine, whiskey, lemons, cheeses, crackers, pies, pastries, cigars, and oysters in season.

They sat around innumerable campfires and sang and cracked jokes. A favorite was about the young recruit who was lonesome and scared and threatened to go home. His sergeant sent him to see the company commander, who told him he was acting like a baby. "I wish I were a baby," he answered, "and a girl baby at that."

Wrapped in their blankets, while the lonesome cry of the whippoorwill echoed through the night, they wondered about the loneliness of life there on the Virginia peninsula, and about when the war would end, and what the folks at home were doing, and what it would be like in Richmond when they got there. In their faith and innocence they didn't even consider the possibility of the Rebels stopping them.

A Contrast of Generals:
Fighting Lee
and Politicking McClellan

When the Confederates withdrew from Seven Pines the afternoon of June 1, Davis, who was on the field as usual, was annoyed and disappointed, as was Lee, his chief military advisor. In their view the attack had been badly bungled. Davis then made a fateful and historic decision on the spot. Effective immediately, he placed Lee in command of the Southern forces. Lee promptly named his new command the Army of Northern Virginia—a name destined for fame in the annals of the Civil War.

Seeing the disorganization and confusion on the field, Lee made no attempt to launch another attack. What he needed now was time to reorganize, time to work out the details of a plan already beginning to form in his mind, and time to put it into operation. Every day McClellan delayed now would be worth a regiment to him.

As the first part of his plan, Lee put his men to work digging the elaborate system of entrenchments that would eventually encircle Richmond completely. For this he was ridiculed by both the press and his own men. His earlier failure in western Virginia was brought up again, and the troops now scornfully dubbed him "King of Spades" and "Ole Spade Lee." They wanted to fight, not dig. Unknown to them, however, Lee was planning more than a static defense. He was well aware of the fact that he could not fight McClellan's type of battle and win; he had neither the equipment nor the manpower. But when the time came, these fortifications could be held by a relatively small number of troops while he massed the bulk of his forces for a counteroffensive. He was familiar with and believed in Napoleon's maxim: "To maneuver incessantly, without submitting to be driven back on the capital which it is meant to defend. . . ."

And "Stonewall" Jackson in the Shenandoah Valley was also part of Lee's plan. Although Jackson was technically under Johnston's command, it had been Lee, working closely with President Davis, who had actually planned Jackson's strategy to keep threatening Washington in an attempt to prevent McDowell's joining McClellan. Lee had written Jackson: "Whatever movement you make, do it quickly, and create the impression, as far as possible, that you design threatening the Washington line." Lee's strategy, combined with Jackson's brilliant tactics, succeeded admirably. As McDowell wrote disgustedly: "If the enemy can succeed so readily in disconcerting all our plans by alarming us first at one point then at another, he will paralyze a large force with a very small one." That is exactly what Jackson succeeded in doing. But now Lee was writing Jackson "to be prepared to unite with the army near Richmond."

Lee believed he knew McClellan, and was therefore fairly certain of the tactics the Federal commander would employ. He was never more right. While McClellan was informing his wife that he intended "to make the first battle mainly an artillery combat," and that as soon as he gained possession of Old Tavern he would "push them in upon Richmond and behind their works . . . bring up my heavy guns, shell the city, and carry it by assault," Lee wrote Jackson: "Unless McClellan can be driven out of his entrenchments he will move by positions under cover of his heavy guns within shelling distance of Richmond."

It was uncanny—almost as if Lee had read the Young Napoleon's letter to his wife. The significance of this can be appreciated fully only when it is remembered that McClellan also wrote that "Lee will never venture on a bold movement on a large scale." In other words, while Lee knew exactly what McClellan's plan was, McClellan did not have the faintest idea of Lee's intentions. To go into battle under these circumstances was to court disaster.

Realizing he would have to get the Federal army out from behind its entrenchments to disrupt McClellan's plan, Lee reasoned the best way to do that was to attack the Federal line of communications to White House on the north side of the Chickahominy. For this to succeed, however, he needed to know the exact position and approximate strength of the Federal right wing guarding that supply line. For this important reconnaissance he selected General J.E.B. ("Jeb") Stuart, the picturesque and cavalier 29-year-old cavalry commander. On June 11 Lee ordered Stuart "to make a secret movement to the rear of the enemy . . . to gain intelligence for the guidance of future operations." Then, remembering the impetuous Stuart as a cadet when he was superintendent of the Military Academy, Lee cautioned him "not to hazard unnecessarily your command or to attempt what your judgment may not approve."

In the cool, predawn darkness of June 12 the sharp, clear notes of "Boots and Saddles" sounded in the Confederate cavalry camps. A picked group of 1,200 officers and men from the First, Fourth, and Ninth Virginia Cavalry and the Jeff Davis Legion, carrying 60 rounds of ammunition and three days' rations per man, moved off at a smart trot in a column of fours down the Brook turnpike in a northwesterly direction. Colonel Fitz Lee (General Lee's nephew) commanded the First Virginia, Colonel "Rooney" Lee (General Lee's son) the Ninth, with the elements of the Fourth divided between them. The two squadrons of the Jeff Davis Legion were commanded by Lieutenant Colonel W. T. Martin. Clanking along in the rear was a section of the Stuart Horse Artillery under Lieutenant James Breathed, a 12-pound Blakely rifle, and a 12-pound howitzer. Expert horsemen, superbly mounted, led by the colorful Stuart with his turned-up felt hat and ostrich plume, elaborate yellow silk sash, heavy jack-boots and gold spurs, they exemplified the debonair, fighting spirit of the South at this early stage of the war.

No one but Stuart knew their destination or mission. When his adjutant asked how long he would be gone, Stuart laughingly replied, "It may be for years and it may be forever." By taking a northwesterly direction he hoped to create the impression the column was heading into the Valley to reinforce Jackson. But late that afternoon, at a safe distance from Richmond, they turned sharply to the east and encamped that night just west of Hanover Court-House. Not until the next morning did Stuart inform his regimental commanders of the object of the mission.

At Hanover Court-House the next morning the column encountered a company of the Fifth U.S. Cavalry patroling the road from Old Church. The Federal troopers quickly withdrew, but kept the Confederate cavalry under observation. They also sent word back to the squadron commander, Captain Royall, at Old Church. Stuart continued on his way, however, heading for Old Church via Taliaferro's Mill and Enon Church to Hawe's Shop. About a mile this side of Old Church the leading regiment, the Ninth Virginia, came upon Captain Royall's squadron drawn up in battle formation waiting for them. Stuart immediately ordered the charge sounded, and in a short, sharp skirmish the Federal detachment was broken and scattered by the charging Confederate troopers.

Fitz Lee, commanding the First Virginia, now galloped up and begged Stuart to allow him to charge his old outfit (the Fifth U.S. Cavalry was formerly the Second U.S. Cavalry commanded by General Lee). Stuart readily consented, and the First Virginia charged into the Federal camp at Old Church only to find its quarry had retreated down the Cold Harbor road to the protection of Union infantry camps.

Stuart had now reached the point of no return. Two courses were open to him. He could continue on in rear of the Union army, cross the Chickahominy, and return to Richmond along the James River; or he could return the way he had come by Hanover Court-House. He reasoned that as the Federals would undoubtedly expect him to take the latter route, to continue on would be the safest policy. He did not believe infantry could catch him and he felt more than "able to whip any cavalry force" that might be brought against him.

Actually, this daring scheme had been in Stuart's mind from the beginning; it appealed to his romantic notion of how the cavalry should operate. The idea had been implanted in his mind by one of his civilian scouts, a young lawyer named John S. Mosby. Mosby had convinced him that as the Union right and rear was protected by only a thin screen of cavalry, a raid around the entire army was feasible. So, after destroying what they could not carry away, the dusty troopers continued on.

The gods of war were smiling on "Jeb" Stuart.

When Captain Royall first received the message about the Confederate advance, he immediately dispatched a rider to inform General Philip St. George Cooke, a commander in the Cavalry Reserve with headquarters at Gaines's Mill on the Mechanicsville road. (It was ironic, perhaps, that Cooke was Stuart's father-in-law.) Cooke ordered the cavalry alarm "To Horse" sounded at once and dispatched six squadrons of the Fifth and Sixth U.S. Cavalry to Royall's relief, followed by the Sixth Pennsylvania Cavalry (Rush's Lancers) and the First U.S. Cavalry. They reached the vicinity of Old Church just about an hour after Stuart's column had departed, but then received orders from Cooke to hold their position. Fortunately for Stuart, an excited junior officer reported to Cooke that he had seen three or four infantry regiments with the Confederate column. Cooke chose to believe the hysterical report from the young, inexperienced officer, despite the protests of experienced men that there was absolutely no evidence of infantry having passed that point. Consequently, on Cooke's request, a brigade of infantry and a battery of artillery, under Colonel Gouverneur Warren, were temporarily assigned to his command and ordered to proceed to Old Church to join the cavalry impatiently waiting there for orders.

Although he had received the first notification from Royall about three o'clock that afternoon, Cooke did not reach the vicinity of Old Church until eleven that night, just a half-hour before Warren's infantry arrived. And it was not until 4 A.M. the next morning that he finally made up his mind to move out after Stuart, and then, despite the violent protests of Warren, he refused to move without the infantry. Not only had he given the Confederates a vital 12-hour start, he now insured the complete success of Stuart's mission by tying his cavalry to the marching pace of the foot soldier.

So Stuart moved on unmolested, burned two transports and some wagons at Garlick's Landing on the Pamunkey, captured a wagon train at Tunstall's Station on the Richmond and York River Railroad, cut communications to White House, crossed the swollen Chickahominy near Forge Bridge, and returned to Richmond June 15 with 165 prisoners and 260 captured horses and mules, having lost only one man in the process.

That Sunday morning Richmond rang with cheers as Stuart's muddy troopers, dirty, unshaven, half-asleep in their saddles, returned to their camps. Years later Colonel John S. Mosby wrote: "The great result of the raid was not in prisoners and property captured, nor in the information obtained, but in the electric effect it produced on the morale of the army."

Mosby's point should not be overlooked. Many historians have tended to deemphasize the importance of the raid on the assumption that it actually helped McClellan more than Lee by alerting the Federal commander to the exposed condition of his line of communications. However, this does not take into account this element of morale, or *esprit de corps*, so necessary for a successful military movement. And it should be remembered that Lee, as a field commander, was an unknown factor at this time. Generally regarded as a conservative engineering officer, there were many people in official positions who believed he lacked the boldness and daring so necessary for a successful field operation. This feeling applied particularly to brigadiers and lower line officers— men such as General Robert Toombs, who believed that West Pointers generally were good for throwing up lines of sand but useless for pushing out lines of battle. To the newspapers Lee was still "Evacuating Lee," while to the enlisted men, who had done nothing but dig entrenchments and drill since Seven Pines, he was still "Ole Spade Lee." Stuart's ride around the Federal army changed all that. Not only had Lee shown his contempt for Mc-Clellan and his army by this bold and romantic stroke, he had also risked the lives of his son and nephew in the process. For a man like that there were many who were willing to fight and die with unquestioning loyalty.

The information obtained by Stuart was, of course, of immense value. Lee now knew the exact disposition of the Federal right wing and its approximate strength. He knew that the high ridge along the Totopotomoy Creek, just north of McClellan's right wing, was not fortified. And there was no indication as yet that McClellan intended to change his base of operations to the James River. So Lee's plan was not only feasible, it was the most practical thing to do under the circumstances. All that remained now was to work out the specific details. The day after Stuart made his report Lee informed Jackson that "the sooner you unite with this army the better." On June 17 Jackson left the Valley and started his forces on the long march to join Lee.

And so Lee planned quietly and prayed for time, while his men drilled and marched, dug fortifications, played cards, sang and listened to bands, visited friends and relatives, or went into Richmond to have a last gay fling. And there was much to see and do in the city. The seventy-two prewar saloons had increased to an unknown number, with such romantic names as Secession Club, Manassas Hall, and Chickahominy Saloon. There were also innumerable gambling halls, billiard parlors, cock-fighting dens, and houses of "ill repute" for the entertainment of the visiting soldiers. Band concerts in Capitol Square were frequent, and the theaters were very popular. Parties in private homes reached an all-time high, with charades, dancing, music, and card playing the most popular activities.

Measles and mumps were rampant in the camps, mostly among the country boys who had never been exposed as the city boys had. The new recruits, who had been afraid ever since Manassas that the war would be over before they could get into it, were impatient for a fight. Others, who had been at Yorktown and Seven Pines, were not so anxious. One Texan remembered: "We found out that the Yankees would fight, and were not to be driven with pop guns, as we were told when we joined Magruder's army at Yorktown." Although they could not know it, with Lee in command the fighting had just begun.

While Lee was preparing to fight what he knew would be a

long, protracted war, McClellan was wondering whether there need be any war at all. Indeed, he believed that the South had seceded from the Union merely because its leaders had misunderstood the intentions of the Lincoln administration—a misunderstanding which could easily be set right; so he dispatched his aide-de-camp, Colonel Thomas Key, on a mission of peace.

That same Sunday morning that Stuart and his men were riding in glory through the streets of Richmond, Colonel Key and a squad of cavalrymen sloshed their way slowly along the narrow, winding road from Cold Harbor to Mechanicsville, their bright blue and yellow uniforms hidden beneath glistening ponchos. It had rained all night and the road was fetlock deep in mud.

Usually on Sundays most of the Federal soldiers could forget, temporarily at least, about marching in the muck. McClellan always liked to give his men a holiday on Sunday if possible—and most of the time he seemed to find it possible, although nonmilitary minds in Washington might wonder how—and they were quick to take advantage of the opportunity to relieve the monotony of guard mounting, inspection, drilling, reviews, ditchdigging, and bridgebuilding.

But to Colonel Key and his cavalry escort it was just a regular duty day. Passing Gaines's gristmill, the troopers noticed some men from the Sixteenth New York unloading corn, and a few members of the Ninety-Sixth Pennsylvania disinterestedly shucking it. When they reached the village of Mechanicsville, they wheeled left into the turnpike past a crude sign reading "Five Miles To Richmond" that some company wag had nailed to a tree. Ahead of them the road ran straight down the gentle slope, like a dirty brown ribbon, to where it crossed the Chickahominy a half-mile away at the Mechanicsville bridge, then climbed another hill and disappeared into the outskirts of Richmond. On either side of it across the river the slopes bristled with heavy cannons protected by thick mounds of earth, like fresh ugly scars on the bright green landscape.

Mechanicsville itself was just a sleepy hamlet, a handful of houses scattered carelessly about a country crossroads, but to Colonel Key and his troopers it must have looked more like a permanent army camp, which is what it was in a way, even if its

permanency was not very definite. Three weeks before a few
Maine and New York regiments had chased two Georgia regiments down the turnpike and across the Chickahominy, and now
Mechanicsville was garrisoned by New Jersey boys. They had
stripped all the usable lumber from the shell-shattered and bullet-
torn barns and houses to make floors for their "dog-tents," while
the latecomers ingeniously spread canvas over the remaining
foundations in forlorn attempts to keep dry.

One impressive brick building, set back amidst a fine stand
of old oak trees, had not been damaged severely and was being
used as a hospital. Honeysuckle and woodbine trailed up the
trelliswork porch. Picturesque oyster shell walks led up to and
around it. From Richmond to here had been a favorite drive of
courting couples. To the cool shade of the spreading oak trees
they had come to enjoy lager beer, fragrant cheeses, and succu-
lent oysters fresh from the nearby York and Pamunkey rivers.

The beer and oysters were long gone, of course, but a steady
pilgrimage still made its way to Mechanicsville daily, only now
they were soldiers in blue. A short distance west of the beer
garden was the favorite spot. From a clearing in back of the oak
trees a lone church spire could be seen pointing over the hill
directly in front across the Chickahominy. That spire was part of
the Confederate capital, and thousands of Federal soldiers came
for a glimpse of the promised land. For most of them it was the
only part of Richmond they would ever see. Even McClellan
paid it a visit. And on that Sunday morning there wasn't a soldier
in the army who would have believed that that was as close to
Richmond as "Little Mac" would ever get.

But Colonel Key's party had not come on a sight-seeing mission. Breaking out a white flag, they proceeded down the pike
towards the broken bridge.

In the dismal swamps bordering the river the pickets watched
their approach with mixed emotions. Always curious about the
actions of officers from headquarters, these New Jersey boys were
also a little apprehensive about what such a high-ranking officer
was doing so far from the main line. Picket duty in the Chickahominy swamps was just about the worst detail a man could
draw, but in the past several weeks a system had been worked out

Federal Pickets in the Chickahominy Swamps

which made it almost bearable. The Union troops had an agreement with most of the Confederate pickets on the other side of the Chickahominy not to fire on each other, as their job, as they saw it, was just to watch the bridge and the approaches to it. This enabled them to make plank walks to their posts and build little platforms so they wouldn't have to lie all day in the mud of the stinking swamps. And this way they could exchange newspapers, whiskey, coffee, and sundry other things, to relieve the tedious monotony of their thankless jobs. Once in a while, of course, it might not work that way, as one Confederate picket warned a New Jersey man. "The man that comes on after me I'll tell not to shoot, and he won't; and you do the same with your relief. But the fellow what comes next, look out for him—he's a damned Louisianian." So the pickets had a fairly comfortable arrangement, and now they were afraid this headquarters officer might put a stop to it.

But Colonel Key was not interested in the pickets' problems.

He dismounted at a little shanty just a few feet from the bridge, planted his white truce flag, and ordered his escort to wait. The shanty had been built by the soldiers on duty and was used as a shelter by the reserve pickets. The colonel found it occupied by Captain Jewett of the Fourth New Jersey and abruptly ordered him and the soldiers out. Overawed and outranked, the captain obeyed, but he immediately notified his regimental commander.

A few minutes later a figure clad in a gray frock coat and trousers, with a huge bushy brown beard, crossed the broken bridge on a plank from the south side of the river and entered the shack.

When Colonel Simpson, commanding the Fourth New Jersey, arrived, he was furiously indignant to find a parley going on with a Confederate officer within his lines without his knowledge or consent. His indignation would accomplish nothing, however. The staff officer from headquarters had already openly insulted the brigade commander, General Taylor, by refusing to disclose his purpose or to ask the general's permission, and Taylor had returned to his tent in disgust. Now Colonel Simpson would try to find out what was going on.

Entering the shack, he interrupted the conference and introduced himself. "Colonel Simpson, Fourth New Jersey Volunteers, general field officer of the day, in charge of pickets."

"Colonel Key, of General McClellan's staff. I am here holding a conversation with General Howell Cobb, to whom permit me to introduce you."

Shaking hands, Simpson remarked with surprise, "Formerly, general, I believe, Secretary of the Treasury."

"Yes," answered Cobb, "I once held that position."

"Why, general, I really did not at first recognize you. You have become so metamorphosed by your beard that I could not identify you."

"We all seem to be fighting under masked faces," replied the Georgian drolly.

Not sure that he understood the remark, and sensing that his presence was unwelcome to Key, Simpson excused himself and joined the waiting escort. If this was just a conversation to discuss the exchange of prisoners, then why all the secrecy, he wondered.

There was something going on here which eluded and puzzled him.

The conversation inside the shack would have puzzled him even more. Details about a proposed exchange of prisoners were quickly agreed upon, and then Colonel Key got down to the real purpose of his mission. McClellan wanted him to converse with General Cobb on "the general subject of the existing contest." McClellan wanted to know, apparently, upon what terms the Confederate States would agree to end the war, and this without the knowledge or authority of anyone in Washington.

Key began by saying that he supposed by now the Confederate leaders were impressed with the hopelessness of their struggle and the hopelessness of foreign intervention. He went on to state baldly that the Army of the Potomac would enter Richmond the very day it moved against the city. Cobb was quick to reply that they would never take Richmond, unless the Confederates abandoned it.

The Federal officer then tried a different approach. "Everyday's experience," he said, "must show to your intelligent men that your people are fighting their friends; that neither the President, the Army, nor the people of the loyal States have any wish to subjugate the Southern States or to diminish their constitutional rights. . . . I cannot understand the grounds upon which your leaders continue this contest."

If that was an example of the thinking at the Army of the Potomac's headquarters, it was an amazing revelation of the character of the commanding general. The expression "neither the President, the Army, nor the people" clearly implied that the "Army" considered itself separate and apart from both the president and the people; it implied that what the president and people might want the "Army" might not want, and vice versa.

Bluntly, then, Cobb informed Key that the "election of a sectional President, whose views on slavery were known to be objectionable to the whole South, evinced a purpose on the part of the Northern people to deprive the people of the South of an equal enjoyment of political rights. We cannot now return without degradation or with security. We must become independent or conquered."

Key replied, "The slavery question has been settled. It is abolished in the District and excluded from the Territories. As an element of dissension, slavery cannot again enter into our national politics. The President has never gone beyond this in an expression of his views; he has always recognized the obligation of the constitutional provision as to fugitive slaves, and that slavery within and between the slave States is beyond Congressional intervention. Such is the political creed of the great body of the Republican party."

If these unrealistic statements, which revealed a startling ignorance of the political situation as well as a juvenile attempt by the "Army" to define the policies of the administration, surprised the man who had been considered for the presidency of the Confederate States, he did not show it. He merely reiterated that the South would ultimately succeed and that the fight had just begun.

With that the conference broke up and Key rode back up the hill to Mechanicsville with Colonel Simpson, who had waited outside until the four-hour meeting was finished. In the course of the conversation, Key remarked that it was originally intended to hold the meeting at Dr. Garnett's, inside the Confederate lines, but that the other side had objected. "Yes," replied Simpson bitterly, "they object to our holding conversations with them within their lines, while we permit Mrs. Lee and family to go all through ours,* and now we allow Howell Cobb to come to hold a conversation within our lines."

Ignoring the obvious sarcasm in Simpson's answer, Key then remarked musingly, "Those leaders on the other side talk as if they would fight."

"Why, who," asked the amazed Simpson, "ever doubted it?"

Coming from an aide-de-camp to the commanding general, it was indeed an amazing statement, particularly considering the fact that the Confederates had fought the Union army at Yorktown and Williamsburg in its march up the peninsula, and just two weeks previously had fallen upon it with great fury at Seven

---

* Mrs. Lee, who had been staying at White House on the Pamunkey River when the Federals overran it, was allowed to pass through the Federal lines on her way to Richmond.

Pines and killed and wounded more than 5,000 of its members. Howell Cobb later would state sarcastically, "Only two things stand in the way of an amicable settlement of the whole difficulty; the landing of the Pilgrims and original sin." President Davis as early as 1861 had remarked publicly that it would undoubtedly be a long, hard war. General Lee had written, "I foresee that the country will have to pass through a terrible ordeal." "Jeb" Stuart had informed his officers that "the war is going to be a long and terrible one. We've only just begun it, and very few of us will see the end."

There were those on the Union side who believed this also. General U. S. Grant, fighting the war in the west, wrote, "I give up all idea of saving the Union except by complete conquest." Another general, William T. Sherman, wrote more dramatically, "The country will be drenched in blood." And it was recorded that President Lincoln told a group of ladies visiting the White House, "General McClellan thinks he is going to whip the Rebels by strategy; and the army has got the same notion. They have no idea that the war is to be carried on and put through by hard, tough fighting, that it will hurt somebody; and no headway is going to be made while this delusion lasts."

Of all the men in high official positions, only McClellan, it seemed, could not appreciate this fact. There always seemed to be a doubt in his mind that the enemy would fight. Although he talked and wrote continuously of being "on the eve of one of the great historic battles of the world," he usually qualified the remark by adding that "the indications are not now that the enemy will fight." The most confusing thing about this is that many times both remarks would be in the same letter or report. All the way up the peninsula his letters and reports contained the same contradictions. On May 12 he informed his wife, "They will fight me in front of Richmond, I am confident." But apparently he was not *too* confident because a few days later found him telling her that it was "very difficult to divine whether secesh will fight a great battle in front of Richmond or not. . . ." Again, "I think one more battle will finish the war." But the next day he confessed he found it "difficult to judge whether the war will soon be at an end or not." In a long report to the president he declared emphatically: "All my information from every source accessible to me establishes the fixed purpose of the rebels to defend Richmond against this army by offering us battle with all the troops they can collect from east, west, and south, and my own opinion is confirmed by that of all my commanders whom I have been able to consult." Then, in the very next paragraph, he baldly states, "It is possible that Richmond may be abandoned without a serious struggle. . . ." It is no wonder that Lincoln was confused, angry, and frustrated.

Colonel Key, in his official report on the conference, added his opinion that "the rebels are in great force at Richmond, and mean to fight a general battle in defense of it. . . ." A week later McClellan was still writing his wife that it looked to him "as if the operations would resolve themselves into a series of partial attacks rather than a great battle."

McClellan forwarded Key's report to the Secretary of War with the request that it be laid on the president's desk for his consideration. At first glance this would appear to be either sheer stupidity or sophomoric political naïveté on McClellan's part. It was neither.

In McClellan's mind he was merely carrying out his God-given duty of saving the country, and this meant more than just winning battles. To him there was nothing inconsistent in the fact that he, a known Democrat with presidential ambitions and Democratic friends in and out of Congress, without authority sent an officer to confer with the enemy on the terms of surrender and to explain to that enemy the policies and objectives of a Republican administration. This was because McClellan apparently did not hold himself accountable to either the president or the Congress; he believed that God had chosen him personally for this great work. "I feel sure that God will give me the strength and wisdom to preserve this great nation," he wrote. "I feel that God has placed a great work in my hands." Consequently, he regarded interference or advice from any source as morally wrong and designed merely to thwart him in his holy mission. "The people call upon me to save the country," he be-

76

THE PENINSULA CAMPAIGN

lieved. "I must save it, and cannot respect anything that is in the way." This included the president, the cabinet, the Congress, and other generals.

When the Secretary of War telegraphed him that Key's report had been given to the president, and then went on to say, "I will only remark now that it is not deemed proper for officers bearing flags of truce in respect to the exchange of prisoners to hold any conferences with the Rebel officers upon the general subject of the existing contest or upon any other subject than what relates to the exchange of prisoners," McClellan did not take the hint. This was merely another example of interference by the administration to keep him from saving the country. Three weeks later he would write another long letter to the president telling him not only how the war should be conducted, but how the country should be governed. McClellan, it seemed, just could not learn from experience.

Beginning
of the Seven Days:
Mechanicsville

Outwardly, at least, McClellan did not seem to be too upset at the Confederate raid around his entire army, although it should have been embarrassing. And to the casual observer and officials in Washington, he appeared to take no significant action, despite the fact that the ride had proved the exposed condition of his line of supply and the tactical weakness of his right flank. There were now two possible courses of action open to him: he could fortify the Totopotomoy ridge and reinforce his right wing, which now consisted mainly of Porter's Fifth Corps stretching from Grapevine Bridge to the Meadow Bridges west of Mechanicsville along the north bank of the Chickahominy; or he could withdraw all his force south of the river and change his base from its exposed position on the Pamunkey and York to the James River. He had more than enough time to do either. Of course, the latter move would be a tacit admission that Lincoln had been right all along in requesting that the army take some action along the line of the James.

The fact is, however, that McClellan did neither. Instead, he actually weakened his right flank further by withdrawing all the detached commands that had accumulated north of the river, such as sections of the reserve artillery and cavalry and various housekeeping details, leaving just the Fifth Corps. Much more significant, however, was his order of June 18 to ship 800,000 rations from White House to the James River. In other words, as a result of Stuart's ride McClellan had now decided that if his line of supply was attacked in strength he would change it to the James, rather than defend it or try to advance south of the river against Richmond. This, of course, was the way McClellan's mind worked; he would outmaneuver Lee, rather than risk fighting him. It is highly significant, also, that McClellan neglected to inform Washington of his actions and plans.

Lee, of course, could not be sure what the Federal commander would do if attacked, and he was unaware of the transfer of rations to the James. But after Stuart's report Lee had his infantry feel out the Union line to see if McClellan might have strengthened his right wing. When it appeared that he hadn't, Lee believed he knew what McClellan would do. He expected him to fall back on the Pamunkey and York to protect his supply bases at White House and West Point. Consequently, Lee decided to concentrate his attack on the Union right wing north of the river.

On June 23 Lee called a meeting of the four generals who would be responsible for carrying out that plan—D. H. Hill, "Stonewall" Jackson, A. P. Hill, and James Longstreet—and explained it to them. Lee then did a rather peculiar thing, which he would never do again and which may have had a disastrous effect on the first major battle of the Seven Days; he retired and left his lieutenants to discuss the proposed plan among themselves. In the discussion it became apparent that the time element of the plan hinged on when Jackson could get his men in position. Jackson, who had ridden fifty-two miles in fourteen hours to get there and would have to spend another night in the saddle returning, seemed a little confused, but stated he could be in position early on the twenty-fifth. Longstreet, who apparently realized the problems Jackson would have to contend with better than Jackson did, suggested he make it the twenty-sixth. Jackson agreed. When Lee returned, he was informed of the date they had agreed upon and that they all understood the plan. Lee then sat down and wrote out the battle order, undoubtedly remembering the confusion at Seven Pines caused by the vague, verbal orders, rather than explicit, written ones.

Jackson was to march from Ashland, about 16 miles north of Richmond, on the twenty-fifth, encamping that night at some convenient place west of the Central Railroad. At 3 A.M. on the twenty-sixth he was to advance on the road leading to Pole Green Church towards Cold Harbor and turn Beaver Dam Creek, just east of Mechanicsville, in the process, thus rendering the strong Federal position behind the creek untenable, and continue on towards Cold Harbor. Branch's brigade, of A. P. Hill's division, was to cross the Chickahominy west of Mechanicsville at the area known as Half-Sink, and when Jackson's advance beyond that point was made known to him he would advance east towards Mechanicsville, thereby uncovering the Meadow Bridges for the rest of Hill's division to cross. Hill would move directly upon Mechanicsville, and as soon as the Mechanicsville Bridge was uncovered Longstreet and D. H. Hill would cross, the latter going to the support of Jackson, and the former to the support of A. P. Hill. Then, in echelon, the four commands would sweep down the north side of the Chickahominy with Jackson in advance on the left and Longstreet nearest the Chickahominy in the rear. Stuart's cavalry would protect Jackson's left flank. Meanwhile, Magruder, assisted by General Benjamin Huger, would hold the lines in front of Richmond, at the point of the bayonet if necessary, supported by General Pendleton's Reserve Artillery. If and when the Federal forces in front of them started to withdraw, then Magruder and Huger would attack.

When the plan was submitted to Jefferson Davis, he approved it but questioned the ability of Magruder to hold if McClellan advanced towards Richmond. Lee assured him that "any advance of the enemy towards Richmond will be prevented by vigorously following his rear and crippling and arresting his progress." Con-

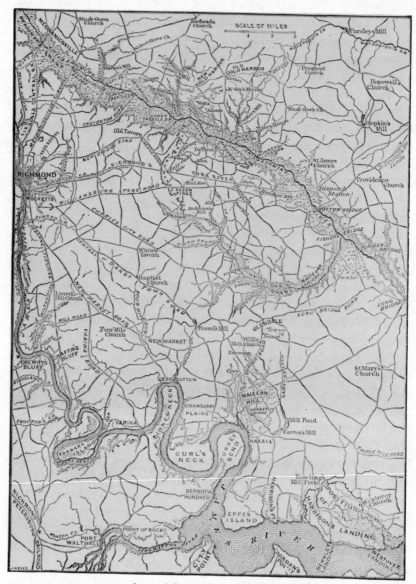

Area of Seven Days Fighting

sequently, his first objective, as he informed Davis, was to "drive the enemy from his positions above New Bridge," about four miles east of Mechanicsville. With New Bridge uncovered, Lee move would be. It would not be a battle, he was careful to ex- rear, in the unlikely event McClellan did elect to march on the city.

It was a gamble, as both men well knew, but if McClellan adhered to his usual tactics, and there was no reason to suppose he wouldn't, then the odds were in Lee's favor. With Jackson's forces from the Valley and reinforcements and recruits from farther south, Lee would have a total force of about 90,000 men. By throwing two-thirds of this force across the river in the attack, he would rely on the remainder to hold the entrenchments in front of Richmond, at least until he could uncover New Bridge and cross to their support.

Every possibility seemed to be covered. All Lee could do now was wait.

McClellan was waiting too, although by this time no one be- sides himself seemed to know why. On June 7 he had telegraphed Washington: "I shall be in perfect readiness to move forward and take Richmond the moment McCall reaches here and the ground will admit the passage of the artillery." On reflection, however, this must have seemed too close to a definite commitment; so three days later he stated there would "be a delay, the extent of which no one can foresee, for the season is altogether abnormal." Under the circumstances, he continued, he wanted to present for the president's consideration "the propriety of detaching largely from Halleck's army to strengthen this. . . ." What the connec- tion was between McClellan's weather and Halleck's army in Mis- sissippi no one in Washington could understand, but it certainly sounded as if McClellan had no intention of attacking Richmond until he eventually had all the troops he wanted. McClellan must have realized that his request might be interpreted that way, because he hastened to add he "wanted it to be distinctly under- stood that whenever the weather permits I will attack with what- ever force I may have."

If this was true it was good news indeed, because on June 12 McClellan reported the weather good and the roads drying rapidly. Two days later he was even more optimistic: "Weather now very favorable. I shall advance as soon as the bridges are completed. . . ." The bridges had not been mentioned in the previous telegrams. Still, McClellan sounded cheerful and optimistic, and, with the weather good, completing the bridges would not be a problem. Of course, he also added that he would "be glad to have whatever troops can be sent me." June 17 the "weather was splendid," which was good news for the president but not for the enlisted men because McClellan discontinued the extra whiskey ration they had been issued in the wet weather.

The weather problem seemed to be settled at last. By June 19 eleven bridges had been thrown across the Chickahominy and the approaches to them corduroyed. McClellan never did explain satisfactorily why he needed eleven bridges in the first place. He certainly didn't need that many just for his supply line. Theoretically, of course, they would enable him to cross the four corps he had south of the river to the north side to reinforce his right

One of McClellan's Bridges Across the Chickahominy

wing, but he definitely had no plans for doing that. Instead, he was planning to change his base to the James, and in that event Porter's corps would have to cross the river. But why one corps would need eleven bridges is another matter. And by June 19 the Young Napoleon had eleven strong redoubts, connected by rifle pits, containing some 70 pieces of heavy siege artillery, including 4½-inch Rodmans and 8-inch mortars, on a 5-mile line from White Oak Swamp on the south to the vicinity of Mechanicsville on the north.

Everything ready—the weather, the roads, the bridges, the artillery. The returns of the Army of the Potomac for June 20 showed that McClellan had 156,838 men, with 127,327 present for duty. What now? Well, now Little Mac wanted to know if he could "expect any new regiments soon?" It seems he had discovered that Lee had sent reinforcements to Jackson in the Valley and this worried him. He dashed off several letters and telegrams to Lincoln and Stanton to see if they knew what was going on. Waiting for answers, of course, took several days. Lincoln's reply was logical: "If this is true it is as good as a re-enforcement to you of an equal force." But that was not the way alarmist McClellan saw it. "If 10,000 or 15,000 men have left Richmond to re-enforce Jackson," he complained, "it illustrates their strength and confidence." Now he couldn't fight the Rebel army until "Providence" permitted, whatever that was supposed to mean. As a cadet at West Point McClellan had been an active and enthusiastic member of the Napoleon Club and he gloried in the title of the Young Napoleon, but apparently he never read the great Bonaparte's statement that "I may lose battles—I do not lose minutes." McClellan was adept at losing whole weeks.

Lee had, in fact, sent reinforcements to Jackson early in June: six Georgia regiments under General Lawton and eight veteran regiments under General Whiting. The idea was to enable Jackson to crush any force in his front if he had to, and then start out for Richmond. In other words, Lee wanted to be sure Jackson joined him even if he had to fight his way out of the Valley. But Lee also shrewdly surmised the effect this might have on McClellan, so he took special measures to be sure the Federal commander would know about the troop movements.

Finally, however, on June 25 McClellan decided what his next move would be. It would not be a battle, he was careful to explain, merely an engineering and artillery affair. He wanted to advance the picket lines on his left in front of the large redoubt on the Williamsburg road so that they would be in position to support an advance on Old Tavern, on the New Bridge road, the next day, or the day after, McClellen wasn't really sure. After all, it might rain or something. He explained to Washington: "I hope to open on enemy's batteries . . . and to gain important advantages within forty-eight hours—not however bringing us to Richmond, but somewhat nearer, and improving our position." Of course, when and if he got to Old Tavern, about a mile in front of his main line, he would have to stop to move up the heavy siege artillery and build new redoubts. But that was all in the unforeseeable future. Right now McClellan had Heintzelman's Third Corps, Sumner's Second, Keyes's Fourth, and Franklin's Sixth—approximately 90,000 men, on a line from White Oak Swamp to Grapevine Bridge. Porter's Fifth Corps, with McCall's division—about 35,000 men—was north of the Chickahominy. On June 23 he informed Porter that if his corps were attacked by superior numbers the other four corps would either support him directly or attack the enemy in their front. When that time came, however, he did neither, and apparently never had any intention of doing so, because the same day he ordered more vessels loaded with provisions and forage to leave White House for the James River.

At eight o'clock on the morning of June 25 General Joseph Hooker's division, of Heintzelman's corps, advanced slowly along both sides of the Williamsburg road in the first action, as it developed, of the Seven Days' battles. General Philip Kearny's division was on the left, or south, of Hooker, covering the left flank of the army down to the western extension of White Oak Swamp, and he was ordered to advance his pickets at the same time in order to protect Hooker's flank. Hooker had Grover's brigade on his left next to Kearny, and Sickles's brigade straddled the Williamsburg road.

A half-mile in front of Hooker the ground was heavily wooded with a belt of swampy soil running through the middle of it. On the far side of the woods was a cleared field extending about 500 yards towards Richmond, across which General Huger's division was posted, with General William Mahone's brigade on the right and General Lewis Armistead's on the left. General A. R. Wright held the center.

Hooker's initial advance drove in the pickets on the Confederate right, south of the Williamsburg road, scattering the Fourth Georgia Regiment in confusion. But when Wright threw in the First Louisiana and the Twenty-second Georgia, Grover's brigade was stopped until Hooker reinforced it with the Fifth New Jersey, and the advance continued. Sickles, driving along both sides of the road, hit Wright's center hard in a sharp skirmish and drove it back. Wright then brought up Ransom's brigade and checked the Federal advance. When the Seventy-first New York, in the center of the line, gave way under pressure, despite the personal efforts of Sickles to rally it, Palmer's brigade from Keyes's corps, with a section of the reserve artillery, came up and stabilized the situation. It was now late afternoon. McClellan, who was on the field, received an urgent message from his headquarters and dashed off after ordering all offensive action to cease.

Both sides claimed a victory in this small affair, known to the Confederates as the battle of King's School-House and to the Federals as the battle of Oak Grove. Federal casualties were about 600; Confederate about 400. Although the end result was that Hooker had advanced his picket line about 500 yards, McClellan's telegram gave the impression that a very important strongpoint had been occupied. This was sent from the field. When he reached his headquarters an hour later, however, and received intelligence that Jackson's force was approaching from the Valley, he became almost hysterical. He informed Washington that Jackson would probably attack his right and rear, and that the Rebels now had a force of 200,000 men. Then, in a burst of insubordination, he declared: "I am in no way responsible . . . I have not failed to represent repeatedly the necessity for reenforcements . . . if the result of the action . . . is a disaster, the responsibility cannot be thrown on my shoulders; it must rest where it belongs." In other words, if by any chance the Federal army won it would be a brilliant victory for McClellan contending against vastly superior forces, but if he lost it certainly could not be his fault, because the secretary of war and the president had not supported him despite his constant pleas for more troops. With both contingencies thus taken care of, in the records at least, McClellan then proceeded to Porter's headquarters across the river to arrange his defenses for Jackson's arrival.

A mile east of Mechanicsville, Beaver Dam Creek wends its sluggish way southward to the Chickahominy through a rather small but sharp ravine. Where the Cold Harbor road crossed the creek, Dr. Ellerson had constructed a millrace and a gristmill. The millrace formed a natural barrier to advancing infantry and a ready-made defense for any force holding the east side of the creek. The only other crossing was a mile north on the Bethesda Church, or Old Church, road. The stream was waist-deep in most places and bordered on both sides by swamps. The only approaches to it from the west were across open fields, down the steep banks of the ravine, and then through the soggy marshlands. It was a naturally strong defensive position, and if properly manned and fortified, unassailable.

When McClellan reached Fifth Corps headquarters later that evening, he found to his satisfaction that Porter had the situation well in hand. McCall's division of Pennsylvania Reserves, attached to the Fifth Corps, was firmly entrenched behind Beaver Dam Creek on about a two-mile front. Seymour's brigade held the heights on the left, from the Chickahominy to just north of the Cold Harbor road; Reynolds's brigade the right, stretching beyond the Old Church Road, sometimes also called the Upper Mechanicsville Road. Meade's brigade was in the rear in reserve. McCall had placed Cooper's battery of six 10-pound Parrotts on the right of the upper road, and Smead's battery of four 12-pound Napoleons on the left. DeHart's battery of six Napoleons was in the center of the line commanding the road from Mechanicsville to Cold Harbor and the adjacent fields. The Fifth Pennsylvania held the crossroads in Mechanicsville, with a few companies of the Thirteenth ("Bucktails") on picket duty along the Chickahominy from Mechanicsville west to the Meadow Bridges. The Eighth Illinois Cavalry patroled the roads north to Hanover Court-House.

McClellan was satisfied. A frontal assault on this position would be military suicide. Yet, admitting as he did that his right flank was somewhat in the air, and realizing that Jackson was approaching from the north, he did nothing to either change or improve his position. There is an old military axiom that states "the strength of a position is measured not by the impregnability of its front, but by the security of its flanks." Stuart's ride had shown conclusively that McClellan's right flank could easily be turned by a force proceeding down the Totopotomoy watershed above the headwaters of Beaver Dam Creek, as McClellan had failed to secure these heights. It was logical to assume, therefore, that if and when Jackson came he would attempt to turn the Federal position at Beaver Dam rather than attack it. The fact that McClellan was aware of the situation but did nothing about it is further proof that his only plan of action, if his line of communication was threatened, was to change his base to the James River. He had no intention of defending his present supply line, let alone of attacking Richmond, even if the opportunity should present itself. Yet he telegraphed Washington: "Every possible precaution is being taken. . . . Nothing but overwhelming forces can defeat us. . . . Have made all possible arrangements." Obviously, he did not subscribe to the theory that attack was the best defense.

And so McClellan, the attacker, rode back through the quiet darkness of the summer night to his headquarters across the river and sat down and waited to be attacked.

Thursday morning, June 26, broke clear and mild, but the first gray streaks of dawn warned of the approach of a scorching sun that would turn the rain-soaked plain, with its myriad streams and swamps, into a steaming cauldron. As the morning wore on, the men of A. P. Hill's division, massed behind the heights overlooking Meadow Bridges, waited expectantly. An impatient, impulsive man, Hill had his men ready to move at four o'clock that morning, with two days' cooked rations in their haversacks, no knapsacks, and only one blanket per man.

Not a big man physically, Hill nevertheless was a picturesque figure with his red shirt, gray flannel jacket, black slouch hat, long, curling hair, and rich red beard. The youngest major general in the Confederate Army at thirty-six, he had roomed with

McClellan at West Point, although graduating a year later in 1847 because of illness, and had courted McClellan's wife when she was Nellie Marcy. Her father, a Regular Army colonel and now McClellan's chief of staff, had not wanted his daughter to have to live on a young officer's pay; so when Little Mac left the army for the railroad business, he also beat his former roommate in the race for her affections.

But now the only thought in Hill's mind was to carry out Lee's plan to destroy McClellan's army. Following the battle order, he had sent General Branch's North Carolina brigade to the area known as Half-Sink, where the Brook turnpike crossed the Chickahominy, about six miles upstream. Branch was becoming impatient also. His men had been under arms and ready to go since before dawn. As Jackson was supposed to start his march from Ashland at 3 A.M. and notify Branch when he had crossed the Central Railroad, Branch reasoned his brigade should be ready to cross the river by 4 A.M. As the sun rose higher in the bright blue sky, Hill apparently became apprehensive that Branch, a former congressman and not a West Pointer, would jump the gun and cross the river without hearing from Jackson. So at eight o'clock he sent an order to his brigade commander reminding him to "wait for Jackson's notification before you move unless I send other orders." An unusual precaution for an impulsive man like Hill.

Finally, at ten o'clock, Jackson notified Branch that the head of his column was just then crossing the Central Railroad. This made the hero of the Valley campaign almost six hours late at that point. But as one footsore veteran of the Thirteenth Virginia explained: "The burning of the bridges and the blockading of the roads by the enemy so impeded our march that we only reached the vicinity of Ashland that night." Jackson had overestimated the marching ability of his battle-scarred men—they had marched over 400 miles and fought 5 battles in the past 40 days—and underestimated the vigilance of Fitz John Porter in blocking the approaches to the Federal position. Withal, these lean, tough fighters were in good spirits. "If the Yanks are as ignorant of this move as we are," they said, " 'Old Jack' has them."

A strange man this Jackson. A strict, almost fanatical Calvinist, uncommunicative to the point of secrecy even with his own staff, trusting no one, yet quoted as saying that he would follow Lee blindfolded. Slow to praise, quick to blame, he had little patience with failure or pomp and ceremony, and was utterly lacking in any sense of humor. Also a classmate of McClellan's at West Point, he was just thirty-eight years old, and without a doubt the leading exponent of Napoleon's theories in either army. It was said of him that as he sat his horse observing a battle, he asked sharply why one of his couriers had not as yet returned from delivering a message. When informed that the man had been killed, Jackson remarked without visible emotion, "Very commendable. Very commendable."

And yet, there was a certain magnetism about the man that made others want to follow him. When he appeared on his dun-colored, sorry-looking sorrel, with his faded uniform and weather-stained Virginia Military Institute cap slouched over one eye, the men cheered. Their enthusiasm stemmed from their faith in his tactical genius and fighting spirit, not from the man himself; no one could love the dour, gaunt Jackson for himself.

Now, however, he was six hours late, unusual for him, but it is evident from his report and his actions that he was not aware of the importance of the time element in Lee's plan. All day his progress was slowed by Federal pickets and skirmishers. Porter had systematically destroyed all bridges and blocked all roads east of Ashland. At the strategic bridge over the Totopotomoy, Jackson delayed long enough to bring up artillery to shell the Federal pickets out of the woods on the far side before he started to rebuild the burned bridge. Then, as he had no "regular pioneers," inexperienced detailed men were assigned the task, necessitating more delay.

Meanwhile, on receipt of Jackson's note, Branch promptly crossed his brigade and disappeared into the woods on the north side of the Chickahominy. As the dust from the marching brigade drifted slowly in the hot, still air, an ominous silence settled over the rest of the army. The day wore on—still nothing but silence, a nerve-wracking, pregnant silence.

McClellan, at his headquarters down the Chickahominy at Dr. Trent's, didn't like it. "All things very quiet on this bank of the Chickahominy," he informed Washington at noon. "I would prefer more noise." With 150,000 men and over 300 pieces of artillery, he should have been able to make all the noise he desired, but that was not McClellan's way.

A. P. Hill would have preferred more noise also. It was now midafternoon, five hours since Branch left, and still no word or sign of action across the river. Hill was gradually coming to the fateful conclusion that he should not wait any longer.

Branch's line of march covered about six miles from Half-Sink to the Meadow Bridges and he should have been able to do that in much less than five hours. But after brushing aside the Federal cavalry pickets near Half-Sink, the brigade ran into three companies of the Thirteenth Pennsylvania Reserves ("Bucktails") at Atlee's Station, and a sharp skirmish ensued. The brigade halted in confusion. The action, however, was too far away to be heard from Meadow Bridges. It was now about 3 o'clock.

And at 3 o'clock Hill lost his patience and threw caution and Lee's plan to the winds.

With no knowledge of either Jackson's or Branch's positions, and without informing his commanding officer, Hill rashly put his division in motion across the Meadow Bridges. Field's brigade headed the column with the Fortieth Virginia in the lead. The other three companies of the "Bucktails," the only Federal force at Meadow Bridges, quickly withdrew, thus inadvertently isolating the three companies holding Branch's brigade at Atlee's Station. Two of them managed to slip between Jackson and Hill and retire to safety, but the third was cut off and captured after spending several days wandering around in the swamps. Hill quickly pushed on towards Mechanicsville.

Lee had climbed up on one of the redoubts along the Mechanicsville turnpike to observe the action. D. H. Hill and Longstreet joined him there. In the distance they could see the gray-clad infantry emerge from the woods on the left, the Federal blue retreating east from the village towards Beaver Dam Creek. But when Hill's men reached Mechanicsville, they came under a heavy fire from the Union artillery behind the creek. This disturbed Lee. If Jackson had turned Beaver Dam the Federals should be withdrawing, and if he hadn't, what was Hill doing in Mechanicsville? Lee mounted Traveller, the big, handsome iron-gray horse with black points that would carry him safely through the Seven Days' battles, and rode down the turnpike to find his divisional commander, while D. H. Hill and Longstreet got their divisions in motion towards the bridge.

On reaching Mechanicsville and coming under a withering artillery fire, Hill decided to hit hard at the Federal right where Jackson should soon be appearing. He sent Anderson's brigade on a wide flanking movement to the left, north of the Old

Lee and Traveller

Church road, while McIntosh's battery tried to keep the enemy occupied. Archer's brigade pushed down the road and then deployed in the open fields to the south, with his left resting on the road. Field formed on his right and extended down to the Cold Harbor road, with Pegram's battery in support. Gregg's brigade was held in Mechanicsville as a reserve. Pender's brigade was not yet up and Branch had not appeared.

As the marching columns went forward the Federal artillery opened with an earth-shaking roar. Seeing the pressure mounting on his right, McCall rushed Kern's reserve battery of 12-pound howitzers over to support Cooper's guns. The flaming cannons tore gaping holes in the Confederate brigades, the shells screaming overhead like a pack of banshees, exploding in clouds of earth, horses, and men. Pegram's battery was quickly cut to pieces, losing forty-seven men and many horses in a matter of minutes, and McIntosh's rendered ineffective. Still they came on, flags flying bravely under the flesh-tearing hail of lead and iron. As the regiments swung out in battle formation across the open fields, the woods on the opposite bank of the creek came alive. From under the trees came the rolling clatter of musketry. A

Confederate Charge at Beaver Dam Creek

dark cloud of smoke floated upward, blotting out the late afternoon sun. The gray lines staggered and slowed as men fell like
leaves in an autumn wind. But Anderson's leading regiment, the
Thirty-fifth Georgia, ably supported by the Fourteenth and
the Third Louisiana Battalion, somehow managed to keep going,
slid down the bank, and wallowed across the swampy stream.
Here they were met by the devastating fire of the "Bucktails"
and two companies of Berdan's Sharpshooters on the right, the
Fifth Pennsylvania in the center, and the First and Second on the
left, supported by the Fourth Michigan and four companies of
the Fourteenth New York. The steel ramrods clashed and
clanged as cartridges were rammed down smoking barrels. Muskets were jerked to the shoulder and fired without aim into the
dense smoke, as the gray ranks floundered helplessly in the thick
morass. As the smoke slowly eddied away, the remnants of the
Confederate regiments could be seen retreating back up the steep
bank. The fire then grew intermittent and weaker as the attack
on the Federal right sputtered and died.

Pender's brigade having come up by this time, Hill sent him in
to support Field on the right in an attempt to turn the Federal
left down near the Chickahominy. But as the column advanced
on the Cold Harbor road and turned south into the open field, it
came under a withering artillery fire from Easton's battery and a
section of Cooper's, stationed on the heights in the vicinity of
Ellerson's Mill, where the Cold Harbor road crossed the creek.
The destructive fire broke the column, and Pender lost control of
his brigade. His leading regiment, the Sixteenth North Carolina,
veered to the left and became mixed in with Field's regiments,
not rejoining Pender until the fight was over. The Thirty-fourth
North Carolina, supposed to support the Thirty-eighth, went too
far to the right, thus leaving only the Thirty-eighth to make the
assault at the mill. Bravely, but hopelessly, the Thirty-eighth
advanced to within a hundred yards of the Union rifle-pits before
the murderous fire of the Twelfth Pennsylvania forced a bloody
withdrawal.

McCall, anticipating a stronger attempt to turn his left,
quickly reinforced it with the Seventh Pennsylvania and Ed-
wards's battery of six 3-inch rifles. Porter sent up Martindale's

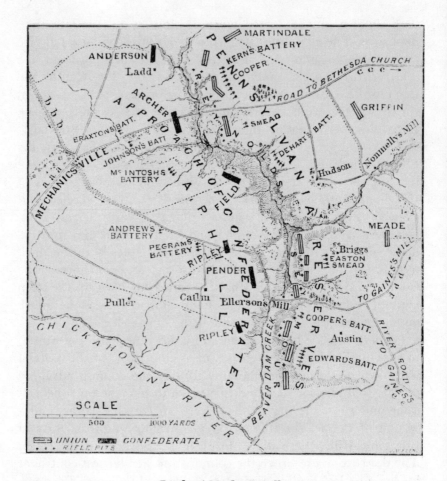

Battle of Mechanicsville

and Griffin's brigades, but they were held in reserve and did not enter the engagement.

The shadows on the field lengthened now as the blazing sun went down. Despite the hopelessness of the situation, Lee decided to gamble in a last desperate attempt to turn the Federal left before darkness set in. He ordered Ripley's brigade, the first of D. H. Hill's division to cross the Mechanicsville Bridge, to move quickly to Pender's support. Jefferson Davis, also on the field in his usual role of general without portfolio, so to speak, issued a similar order, unknown to Lee. Ripley, however, instead of proceeding to the extreme right to outflank the Federal artillery, advanced over the same exposed ground the Thirty-eighth North Carolina had used, and attacked the strong position directly in front of Ellerson's Mill, where he was literally cut to pieces. Of the 575 casualties suffered by the brigade, the Forty-fourth Georgia alone sustained 375. Darkness then mercifully put an end to the hopeless assaults.

The battle, of course, should never have been fought. It was a military zero so far as Lee was concerned. He had suffered about 1,500 casualties and achieved absolutely nothing. A high percentage of those casualties were company-grade officers and regimental staff men—men needed to command the brigades and divisions in the years to come, whom the Confederacy could ill afford to lose. Out of about 14,000 troops engaged, Lee had suffered a 10 percent loss, while Federal casualties amounted to only 391 out of a like amount engaged.

Historians and others have tended generally to blame Jackson for this costly blunder. It is true that Jackson was late and did not actually turn Beaver Dam Creek until the next morning, which seems inexcusable. The reasons for the delay—fatigued troops and Porter's alertness in destroying the bridges, obstructing the roads, and keeping patrols well forward—are just that, reasons; they cannot be used as excuses for his failure to move promptly to his assigned position. But it seems quite apparent from Jackson's official report and his communications at this time that he did not understand his mission as Lee intended it. He also had little knowledge of the area and his maps were almost useless. In his report Jackson stated: "On the morning of the 26th . . . I took up the line of march for Cold Harbor . . . crossed the Central Railroad about 10 A.M." Lee's written order instructed Jackson to "advance on the road leading to Pole Green Church, communicating his march to General Branch. . . ." That is exactly what Jackson did; he notified Branch of his position at 10 A.M. and Branch then moved out. There was nothing in Jackson's orders that stated he was to be in a specified position at a specified time. The only other instruction Lee gave him was to "bear well to his left, turning Beaver Dam Creek and taking the direction toward Cold Harbor."

It will be recalled that at the meeting on June 23 Lee had left the room after presenting his battle plan, something he never did again; so more than likely Jackson's understanding of the plan and the terrain was sketchy, to say the least. It is certainly evident that he did not understand the importance of the time element, or the fact that by his turning Beaver Dam Creek the Federals would have to withdraw rather than stand and fight.

It is also possible that A. P. Hill did not fully understand Lee's idea. He stated in his report: "Three o'clock having arrived, and no intelligence from Jackson or Branch, I determined to cross at once rather than hazard the failure of the whole plan by longer deferring it." But Lee did not intend, nor expect, to fight at Beaver Dam; he was well aware of the natural strength of that position. By Jackson turning it on the north, he believed McClellan would have to withdraw as the position would then be untenable. Also, once he committed his forces to the north side of the Chickahominy, it was vitally important to Lee that he quickly gain control of at least one of the bridges lower down the Chickahominy to enable him to reunite the wings of his army to counter any move McClellan might make. Thus, Hill's moving before Jackson was in position not only endangered Lee's plan; against a commander other than McClellan it could have been disastrous for the whole army. To move or wait for Jackson to reach his assigned position was Lee's decision to make, not Hill's. By not informing his commanding general of the circumstances under which he arbitrarily committed his division to action, Hill, in effect, temporarily deprived Lee of control of his army and the battle. The useless loss of life could have been prevented simply by waiting until Jackson turned Beaver Dam the next morning. McClellan had not moved all day, and by three o'clock in the afternoon it was quite evident that he had no intention of moving; so nothing would have been lost by the delay. Hill's action, of course, deprived Lee of the opportunity for postponement, and at the same time informed McClellan of the Confederate plan of action.

Actually, although Lee could not be sure of it, the element of surprise had been lost before the fight at Beaver Dam. Stuart's ride had taken care of that. And although Lee had taken special

precautions to mask Jackson's move from the Valley, the strategy
had been suspected by the Federals for several days. When the
reinforcements had been sent from Richmond to the Valley, even
Lincoln had asked McClellan, "Have not all been sent to de-
ceive?" And Stanton told him, "We shall have every confidence
in your ability to drive Jackson back. . . ."

Lee's situation was now critical. The advantage of surprise was
no longer his; Jackson's failure upset the important time element
of the plan; and Hill's impulsive action notified the enemy of his
intentions, giving McClellan an opportunity to reinforce his
right wing during the night, or to mount a strong attack against
the defenses of Richmond in the morning. Because of the repulse
at Beaver Dam, Lee had not yet achieved his first objective,
which, according to his battle order, was to "drive the enemy
from his position above New Bridge," about four miles east of
Mechanicsville. His whole plan for the defense of the Confederate capital, in the event McClellan should elect to march on the
city with his main force south of the Chickahominy, hinged on
his ability to cross the river quickly and attack the Federal rear.
Lacking control of New Bridge, Lee could not do so. Realizing
all this, he still decided to try to carry out his original plan. A
lesser man might well have hesitated.

Early next morning, having by then turned Beaver Dam
Creek, Jackson was to continue on towards Cold Harbor, with
Stuart's cavalry protecting his left flank. D. H. Hill would take
the Old Church road from Mechanicsville to Cold Harbor via
Bethesda Church, and join Jackson there. A. P. Hill was instructed to push down the Cold Harbor road towards Gaines's
Mill, while Longstreet, on A. P. Hill's right, would also proceed
to Gaines's Mill on the lower, or River road, which ran generally
parallel to the Cold Harbor road but closer to the Chickahominy.
The immediate objective was New Bridge; the ultimate objective
McClellan's line of communication to White House, thus draw-
ing McClellan out from behind his entrenchments and relieving
the pressure on Richmond.

With his forces committed, his orders issued, all Lee could do
now was wait and hope.

Buying Time for
McClellan's Change of Base:
Gaines's Mill and Savage Station

McClellan was jubilant. "I almost begin to think we are invincible," he wired Stanton at 9 P.M. from Porter's headquarters on the field. He hastened to add, of course, that the victory was "against great odds," although neither Porter nor McCall mentioned anything about "odds" in their reports, and the forces engaged were actually about equal. Significantly, McClellan again neglected to mention anything about a change of base at this time. Yet, a few hours later when Jackson's position had been definitely ascertained, he issued the orders to start the hazardous movement on the long road to Harrison's Landing on the James River. And he telegraphed his wife: "There will be a great stampede, but do not be alarmed . . . You will hear that we are pursued, annihilated, etc. Do not believe it. . . ."

Although 800,000 rations had been sent up the James on June 18, and several other boatloads of forage and provisions on the

98

twenty-third, Colonel Ingalls, in charge of the depot at White House, now had the difficult task of moving over 400 vessels loaded with supplies down the treacherous York River. The numerous wharfs, constructed at great length by lashing canal boats and barges together, had to be broken up; the rolling stock of the railroad destroyed; supplies, that could not be shipped, burned. At the same time millions of cartridges and shells and thousands of tons of supplies were started on the way to Savage Station by rail and wagon, so that the various components of the Army of the Potomac could be replenished when they passed that point on the way to Harrison's Landing. The other two depots on the railroad, at Orchard Station and Dispatch Station, were broken up and these supplies sent to Savage Station also. From the corrals in the vicinity of White House, over 2,500 head of cattle were rounded up and started on their drive to the James in the early morning hours of June 27.

About 2 A.M. that morning Porter received his order to withdraw from Beaver Dam to a new position about a mile in rear of Gaines's Mill, previously selected by General Barnard, McClellan's chief engineer. This could be a dangerous operation, particularly if executed in daylight, but Porter was a cool, efficient fighter. A big man with a full, handsome beard, he had a quick, observant look about him, although inclined to be reserved in his relations with others. A loyal officer and personal friend of McClellan, he graduated from the Military Academy in the class of 1845 and served with distinction in the Mexican War under Scott. Always neat and carefully attired, he ran his military commands the same way, a habit he may have acquired from serving as Lee's adjutant at West Point.

Now, however, his problem was to get the Fifth Corps safely away from Lee's forces. The corps wagons were quickly loaded and sent across the Chickahominy. Commissary and ordnance stores that could not be transported for lack of space were ordered destroyed. The men of Butterfield's brigade, Morell's division, spent the dark hours of the early morning frantically moving the heavy siege guns, at Hogan's and Gaines's farms, to safety across the river. The Eighteenth Massachusetts and Seventeenth New York, both of Morell's division, had been detailed to assist Stoneman's cavalry guarding White House. Fearing for their safety if they tried to rejoin the division, Porter ordered them to stay and withdraw with the quartermaster troops.

When the order to withdraw filtered down to McCall, however, he was not too happy about it, and with good reason. Under cover of darkness he believed the movement could be accomplished without loss or difficulty, but "now it would be daylight before the movement—under fire, one of the most delicate and difficult in war—could be commenced." He ordered Meade's brigade, which had been held in the rear in reserve during most of the battle, to withdraw first, followed by Reynolds, using the tough "Bucktails" to protect his rear, then Seymour on the left, with the Ninth Pennsylvania serving as rear guard.

After the tenseness of a fight the men in the ranks were exhausted—thirsty, dirty, and hungry. Although their casualties had been slight, 391, and the "Bucktails" and Fifth Pennsylvania between them had suffered almost half of that total, they had been fighting for over six hours. When the battle ended about 9 P.M., many of them were out of ammunition and food, but still had to lie with their arms at the ready in the expectation that the attack would be renewed in the morning. Cartridge boxes, haversacks, and canteens had to be filled, weapons cleaned, wounded cared for and removed, the dead buried. It was early in the morning before these necessary chores were completed, and then they started to withdraw.

As the various regiments pulled out of position, the "Bucktails" deployed right and left, as did the Ninth Pennsylvania, in an effort to make the Confederates believe that the line was still strongly held. But as the first thin streaks of dawn changed the landscape from brown to gray, heavy columns of infantry could be seen filling the roads leading to the two fords over the creek. During the night Hill's artillery had moved up to within grapeshot range of the Federal position, and now opened with a roar. Anderson, on the left, advanced down the Old Church road, while Gregg's brigade, in reserve the day before, forced the crossing at Ellerson's Mill, supported by Pender's weary troops. But the road in places was covered with the dead and wounded from the previous unsuccessful assaults, and precious time was used to move them to permit the passage of artillery, and the small bridge, which the Federals had destroyed, had to be rebuilt. It was past eight o'clock before the advance was resumed.

By now the air was stifling. As the Pennsylvanians retreated, the sun blazed down and the dust rose and hung about the men in smothering clouds. Flags hung limp in the shimmering, sultry heat. Men fainted and had to be left by the roadside. Supplies and equipment that could not be moved in time burned fiercely in the fields. Under the pressure of Hill's advancing brigades, the dead and wounded had to be abandoned. A company of the "Bucktails," fighting desperately in the woods and swamps, was finally cut off and surrounded and forced to surrender in a body. But the remainder fell back and joined the Ninth Massachusetts for another delaying action directly behind Powhite Creek at Dr. Gaines's gristmill.

Here Powhite Creek flows in a southerly direction, emptying into the Chickahominy farther south. Where the Cold Harbor road crossed it Dr. Gaines had built his mill, with the banks on either side steep and wooded. Longstreet's division, on the southern end of Lee's line close to the Chickahominy, had crossed the creek about noon and halted, fearing for the safety of his left flank until Hill should come up. About this time Gregg's brigade reached the vicinity of the mill, and finding the Federal rear guard well entrenched, Andrew's battery was brought up to shell the woods and drive them out. Then the First and Twelfth South Carolina were thrown forward to force the crossing. The remnants of the "Bucktails" hastily withdrew, but their mission had been accomplished. They and the Ninth Massachusetts had bought with their lives the time necessary for Porter's Fifth Corps to gain its position behind Boatswain Swamp. Gregg's brigade once again had to rebuild the bridges before the artillery could cross. It was now almost 2 P.M.

Time was running out and the situation for Lee was still critical. To be sure, Longstreet had uncovered New Bridge, but Porter could still control the approaches to it with his heavy guns behind Boatswain Swamp. Longstreet now reported a powerful Federal force behind a naturally strong position in his front, and halted to await further orders. Hill reported a similar situation in his front. Jackson and D. H. Hill, having to take a roundabout road to get to Cold Harbor on Lee's left, were not yet in position. But something had to be done and done quickly, if Lee's plan was to have any chance for success.

The trouble was, though, any attack made quickly would have to be made without reconnaissance of any kind. There would be no way of knowing which part of the Federal line might be weaker than another. There would be no time to become familiar with the topography of the area so that the divisional commanders could use it to their best advantage, or at the least, not let it work to their disadvantage. The Confederate maps were of little help in this respect. As D. H. Hill wrote after the war: "In these battles, the great want of the Confederates, strange as it may seem, was accurate knowledge of the country in their front." Brigade commander Law was even more emphatic. "The real trouble," he declared, "was that the Confederate officers, even those in high command, knew little or nothing of the topography of the country in which they were operating. To undertake the defense of a city, without attempting to learn the topography of the country around it, was a new principle in modern warfare."

The position selected by Barnard and approved by McClellan could and should have been impregnable. Between Grapevine Bridge and New Bridge was an elevated, flat plateau, that rose gently from the Chickahominy to its crest on the north, then curved around in a semicircle from one bridge to the other. A small creek—the natives called it Boatswain Swamp—flowed westerly along the front of the plateau and then turned sharply to the south in a great curving arc, emptying into the Chickahominy a short distance below New Bridge. In some places the creek was bordered by swamps, in others by steep banks thirty to forty feet high. A dark and somber line of trees crowded up these slopes on either side, shutting out the sun. The only approaches to this position were across open fields and down one slope and up the other, or into one swamp and out the other.

On the crest of this partially wooded plateau Porter placed his Fifth Corps in a semicircular line of defense, with both extremes resting near the Chickahominy. Morell's division held the left quadrant and Sykes's division of Regulars the right, with Mc-

Call's weary troops in reserve. Cooke's cavalry was on Porter's extreme left, in the lowlands bordering the Chickahominy, while the artillery was placed in strategic spots along the rim of the plateau. During the course of the impending battle Porter would be reinforced by Slocum's division, giving him a total strength of about 35,000, as opposed to over 60,000 for Lee.

McClellan's situation at this point was also critical, as he well realized. "I look upon today as decisive of the war," he informed Porter. Not, however, decisive in the sense of willingness to match the Army of the Potomac against the Army of Northern Virginia, or in any attempt to march on Richmond. It was decisive only in the sense that McClellan desperately needed time to work out all the complicated logistical problems involved in his change of base in the face of an aggressive enemy. Thousands of wagons had to be loaded and the routes selected; orders had to be written and instructions issued to the various corps commanders; supplies that could not be transported had to be destroyed; arrangements had to be made for gunboats, requested from the Navy, to convoy the supply vessels up the James; passages across White Oak Swamp had to be secured and orders given for obstructing the roads and fords to delay pursuit; the herd of 2,500 head of cattle had to be protected; the reserve artillery had to be escorted; and all these complicated arrangements would have to be made quickly.

To Porter and the Fifth Corps fell the job of buying the time so desperately needed. "You must hold your own until dark," McClellan ordered.

A half-mile east of Gaines's Mill was a crossroads the natives called New Cold Harbor. Here one road went directly south to the Watt farm; another slanted southeast to the Adams place; while the main road continued east for a mile to Cold Harbor, or Old Cold Harbor, then turned sharply south for two miles to Grapevine Bridge.

The narrow, dusty road to the Watt house was bordered by a strip of woods near the crossroads, then led through the open spaces of a cornfield and wheatfield before plunging into the cool shade of the trees crowding up the steep slopes of the banks of Boatswain Swamp. The house itself stood on the edge of the

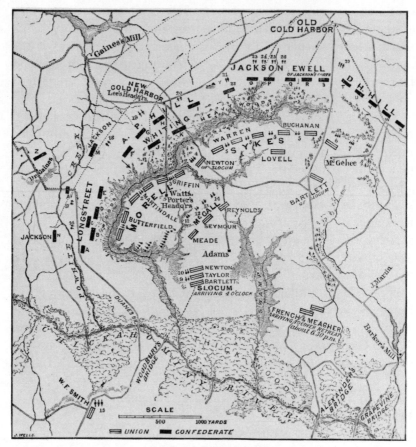

Battle of Gaines's Mill

plateau where it dropped off sharply into the Swamp, about mid-
way between Grapevine Bridge and New Bridge. In the rear the
land sloped gently down to the valley of the Chickahominy. It
was just a plain, square gray farmhouse, not fancy enough to be
called a plantation, typical of its time and place. In the shade of
the woods nearby stood several slave cottages.

Although the land itself had been in the Watt family for over a
hundred years, the house was only about thirty years old. Years
ago the surrounding fields had blossomed white with cotton, the
seeds picked by hand, the fiber carded, spun, and woven, the
fabric bleached and shipped to England to be made into dresses

and returned. The cotton was long gone, of course, and now the fertile fields grew diversified crops to help feed the growing population of Richmond.

In other times, when peace was on the land, the Watts liked to have their many grandchildren visit with them in the slow summer months. Then the woods and hills echoed with merry laughter and innocent voices as the children raced through the peach orchard down the shaded hill for the clear, cold water from the moss-lined, fern-shaded spring; or wandered along the banks of the dark, sluggish Chickahominy gathering mussel shells or stone arrowheads from the mysterious past; or talked to the century-old slave who remembered seeing Cornwallis's redcoats driving off the horses and cattle in the lower fields. Sometimes they made believe they saw Indians through the twilight gloom of the dense foliage among the gnarled and twisted tree trunks.

But now it was Friday, June 27, 1862, and three of the Watt grandchildren were soldiers in the Fifteenth Virginia Infantry. Now the whirlwind of battle was fast approaching. Now the woods would echo to the roar of cannons, the crack of musketry, the angry shouts of men trying desperately to kill each other, the screams of the wounded and dying.

All through the sultry morning the blue-clad troops marched up the dusty road, bayonets flashing in the burning sun, wheeling to the left and right in front of the house to take their positions along the crest of the plateau and on the slopes in the woods. A section of Weeden's Rhode Island battery of 3-inch rifles galloped up and maneuvered smartly into position, unlimbering at the edge of the peach orchard in front of the house. Martin's Massachusetts battery of 10-pound Parrotts swung off the road into the opposite field. Squads of cavalry dashed by, while artillery and ammunition wagons creaked their way through the lower fields. Then McClellan's siege guns began to rumble on the other side of the Chickahominy. Stray cannonballs plowed holes in the lower fields. One tore the roof off the stable and another knocked the top off the kitchen chimney. The slave cook burst out of the house screaming wildly. "Where is Mars Peter? Somebody go find Mars Peter. If they don't stop this foolishness, somebody is gonna git hurt presently."

Federal Artillery at Gaines's Mill

An aide from Porter's staff galloped up in a cloud of dust and informed "Mars Peter" that the house was in the center of the Federal line and would have to be evacuated. Also, Porter wanted it for his headquarters. Mrs. Watt, seventy-eight years of age, was ill in bed and refused to leave her home. But two husky field hands picked her up, mattress and all, and put her in a farmcart with a few personal belongings; and the forlorn party creaked its lonely way to safety through thousands of curious Federal soldiers.

Down in the swampy marshland bordering the Chickahominy on Porter's extreme left, the men in the Forty-fourth New York, Morell's division, decided they needed a little more protection than the swamp, creek, ravine, and woods gave them. They hit on the idea of chopping down some pine trees to dam the creek in their front, making their position almost invulnerable, at least against frontal assaults. Their left flank was protected by the Chickahominy, but on the right there was nothing they could do except rely on the Eighty-third Pennsylvania Infantry. The Pennsylvanians were not so fortunate as the New Yorkers, however; they were short of axes. Still, they did their best, gathering slashings, felled trees, and rubbish and piling them up to form a breastwork of sorts. Farther up the line, in Martindale's and Griffin's brigades, the regiments lacking axes utilized the Watt fences in place of felled trees, plugging the openings between the rails with bales of hay, and, when that was gone, using their knapsacks. Over on Porter's right, Sykes's division of Regulars, plus the Fifth and Tenth New York Volunteers, occupied a ridge that extended to the McGehee farm, east of the Cold Harbor to Grapevine Bridge road, and that commanded the open fields and swamps in front of it. There were few fences here, although the Twelfth U.S. Infantry found a sunken road in front of the McGehee house that was even more effective, and the men were short axes, but a heavy concentration of artillery to sweep the plain in front about made up for the lack of felled trees.

The shortage of axes is one of the forgotten little details in history that sometimes decided the course of battles and even the fate of nations—the old story about a kingdom being lost for the want of a simple nail. Unlike most European armies, in which each corps or division had a company or regiment of engineer troops assigned to it to issue tools when necessary and collect them when the job was done, in the Army of the Potomac at this stage of the war the quartermaster department issued entrenching tools along with all the other supplies. Thus it was impossible to maintain any system of responsibility for the tools. The Civil War soldier found an axe a very handy thing to have in camp, but when the army moved it was usually the last item he thought of, and if by any chance he did take it with him, it was generally the first article to be dropped along the roadside on a long, hot march.

Porter knew his men and what they would do; so after General Barnard had guided him to his assigned position, he requested Barnard to inform McClellan that a large supply of axes was urgently needed. When Barnard reached army headquarters at Dr. Trent's on the other side of the Chickahominy about ten o'clock that morning, he was informed that the commanding general was resting; then, incredibly, he went to his own tent and stayed there until late afternoon instead of delivering the message. The result was, of course, that by the time Porter got the axes they were useless to him.

For some of the Pennsylvanians, however, the oversight was a godsend. Porter had McCall's division on the plain in rear of the Watt house in reserve until late in the battle, and some 200 men of the Eleventh Pennsylvania were detailed to helve the axes when they arrived. As it developed, they were the only members of that ill-fated regiment to walk away from the battle; the others, 684 of them, were either killed or captured.

Despite the lack of axes, Porter was generally pleased with his defensive position. From his headquarters in front of the Watt house he could see the greater part of the field and could communicate readily with all parts of it. His division commanders had their men in two lines, one behind the other, Morell's on the slopes of the ravine above Boatswain Swamp, Sykes's along the crest of the ridge on the right. A line of skirmishers was strung out in front, Morell placing Berdan's Sharpshooters, armed with Sharps breech-loading rifles, on the edge of the wheatfield across the creek. The Fifth Corps was ready for whatever might be coming.

Across the river at Dr. Trent's, McClellan was also well satisfied at the way things were progressing. "The troops on the other side are well in hand," he informed Washington at ten o'clock that morning, "and the whole army so concentrated that it can take advantage of the first mistake made by the enemy." He neglected to explain just how he would go about taking advantage of any mistake. He was not on the field of impending battle and had no intention of going there. It would be up to Porter to decide what action to take, at least in theory, in the event Lee made a mistake, but Porter's hands were tied. He had strict orders that under no circumstances should his men leave their entrenchments to "pursue a repulsed foe." The order applied to the other corps commanders also. Franklin was instructed "not to do anything that might bring on a general engagement," while Heintzelman was told to regard his entrenchments as his "true field of battle." Under these circumstances, Lee could make every mistake in the book and there was nothing any of the corps commanders in the Army of the Potomac could do about it.

By noon, however, McClellan had lost some of his complacency. He warned Washington he was being attacked by Jackson and two other divisions. What it was, of course, was merely A. P. Hill's advance brigade pushing Porter's rear guard at Gaines's Mill, but McClellan took advantage of the occasion to prepare Washington for his planned change of base. "If I am forced to concentrate between the Chickahominy and the James, I will at once endeavor to open communication with you." It is highly significant that he did not inform his superiors at this time that he had already requested the Navy to convoy the supply vessels from White House up the James, and had made preparations to destroy the bridges over the Chickahominy. The point is, in McClellan's mind there was no "if" involved at all; at the very moment he sent the telegram to Stanton he was already in the process of changing his base to the James. But this was something he did not want known, apparently, at least not yet, because if the choice was his, then it followed that the blame—if there was to be any—would rest on his shoulders. But if he waited until Lee hit his right wing hard, which he now knew Lee was going to do, then he believed he could shift the responsibility for the results to Washington. Two days previously he had stated: "If I had another good division I could laugh at Jackson," and now he made certain his government was informed that he was "contending at several points against superior numbers," which, of course, was completely false. But it was in the records now, and that was an important point with George B. McClellan.

To the men in Porter's Fifth Corps, however, none of it was important. The noon sun blazed hot as an ominous silence settled over the area. The growing corn rustled softly in the hot breeze. Behind the bales of hay and the make-shift barricades, in the shade of the trees on the slopes above Boatswain Swamp, the soldiers swore and sweated in their heavy woolen uniforms, waiting for the attack they knew had to come. Large columns of dust swirling high in the sky warned them it would not be long in coming either. But some of them, like soldiers in every war there ever was, fell into the depths of forgetful sleep. Incredibly, newsboys suddenly appeared along the lines, shattering the pregnant silence with their cries of New York and Philadelphia newspapers. A large shipment had just arrived, and these enterprising Yankees wanted to reach their customers while they were still alive and anxious to read.

Then, about two o'clock, came the dull popping of the skirmishers from beyond the trees in their front. Yellow lights began to blink along the regimental fronts, and little balls of smoke, gray and compact, floated gracefully upward in the still, hot air. Minié balls buzzed among the branches and spanged into the trees. Leaves and pine needles showered down softly, like the first light splatter of a sudden summer storm.

It was Gregg's brigade, of A. P. Hill's division, driving in the Federal skirmishers. After chasing off Porter's rear guard at the Gaines's Mill crossing of Powhite Creek, these South Carolinians continued on to the crossroads at New Cold Harbor and then filed into the open field on the left of the Watt house road. Here they came under fire from Sykes's division on the far side of Boatswain Swamp. Gregg reported the Federal forces in his front and requested permission to attack. Hill rejected the idea, however, until the rest of his division could be brought into line. Branch was put in on the right of Gregg with his right resting on the Watt house road; then Anderson, Field, and Archer formed in that order through the wheatfield west of the road. Pender, who cleared the wheatfield of Berdan's Sharpshooters, was then relieved by Archer and put in reserve along the Cold Harbor road behind Gregg and Branch. Hill now waited to hear from Longstreet, who was supposed to come up on his right, connecting with Archer.

Lee had been somewhat surprised that the Federals had not made a stand directly behind Powhite Creek. When Jackson turned Porter's right flank above Beaver Dam, forcing the withdrawal, Lee had believed that McClellan was retreating towards the Union base at White House on the Pamunkey; so his objective was still to sweep down the north side of the Chickahominy to cut the railroad before the enemy could withdraw, uncovering New Bridge in the movement. With Jackson and D. H. Hill advancing on the Old Church road north of Powhite Creek, he had hoped to again flank the Federal army out of its defensive position. Now, however, he realized McClellan's line could not be turned but would have to be broken. Despite the natural strength of the position, Lee believed his situation was critical enough to justify an immediate attack. Because of the repulse at Beaver Dam, he had not yet achieved his first objective, to "drive the enemy from his position above New Bridge."

When all the Confederate divisions came up, Lee would have Longstreet on his extreme right, with his right on the Chickahominy facing east, opposite Morell's left. A. P. Hill would be in the center across the Watt house road, facing generally south, opposite Morell's right and Sykes's left, but attacking slightly southeastward. Jackson, at Old Cold Harbor, would be facing south also, in front of Sykes, with D. H. Hill on his left facing slightly southwestward. Lee still believed that McClellan would try to protect his base and retreat towards White House, and, by the inactivity of the Federal troops in front of Huger and Magruder on the other side of the river, he was convinced that McClellan had reinforced his right wing and that the greater part of the Federal army was now in his front. Naturally he assumed that McClellan would be commanding on the field. On these erroneous assumptions he made his plans.

A. P. Hill would attack the center while Longstreet made a feint on the Federal left. Then when Jackson appeared on the Federal right, Lee believed McClellan would shift part of his troops to meet Jackson's threat in order to keep him from getting between McClellan and his base at White House. As soon as McClellan did this, Longstreet would turn the feint into a full assault, and together with Hill drive the enemy forces into Jackson and D. H. Hill waiting on Lee's left.

It did not work that way, however, mainly because the whole plan was based on a false premise. Lee assumed he knew what McClellan was going to do, but for once the Young Napoleon surprised him. With the basic premise wrong the whole idea was wrong, resulting in a series of uncoordinated attacks that proved to be terribly costly in manpower. It was a calculated risk, of course, and Lee apparently believed his situation to be critical enough to warrant it.

Hill gave the order to advance sometime after 2:30 P.M., but because of poor staff work even this divisional attack was not coordinated properly. Gregg, Branch, and Anderson became engaged, in that order. Branch becoming hard-pressed, Hill sent Pender to his support, and then ordered Field to support Anderson. This left Archer, on the extreme right, unsupported, as he advanced alone across the open wheatfield.

Porter's artillery on the rim of the plateau opened with a terrifying roar, blasting holes in the gray lines as they advanced across the open fields to the edge of the woods bordering Boatswain Swamp. Their own artillery was practically useless; Hill had not massed it for an offensive and succeeded in getting only four batteries into action. Crenshaw's and Johnson's batteries, supporting Gregg and Branch, were quickly cut to pieces. Pegram, who had lost forty-seven men and most of his horses at Beaver Dam, was not much help to Anderson, and Braxton's battery, supporting Archer, was ineffective against the massed Union guns.

But still they advanced, through the smoke across the open fields and into the woods along the creek, only to be met by a sheet of flame as the Federal line exploded into action with a metallic roar. Stopping every few paces to load and fire, the Confederates were perfect targets as they tried to work their way down the slope to the creek by moving from tree to tree. In the hot, still air the smoke clung to the ground before lifting, and through it the muskets flashed and crackled, as the men fired blindly. The thick, sulphurous smoke became suffocating. The line wavered and stopped, as men fell writhing. In the wild confusion of the woods and swamps and smoke and noise, regimental and company commanders lost communication and control. Soon the rolling smoke disclosed men running to the rear, others crouching and cowering behind the trees. Archer and Anderson finally ordered their men to lie down in an attempt to keep them on the field, as some of their regiments broke and ran. The attack fizzled and died as Hill was thrown back with heavy losses.

Longstreet wisely realized that a feint now would not help; so he ordered an all-out frontal assault on the strong Federal line. The attack hit Butterfield's and Martindale's brigades, of Morell's division, on the Federal left, but the same circumstances applied here as in Hill's earlier attack. Longstreet reported: "In front of me the enemy occupied the wooded slope of Turkey Hill, the crest of which is 50 or 60 feet higher than the plain over which my troops must pass to make an attack . . . on the slope of the hill was a line of infantry behind trees, felled so as to form a good breastwork. . . . The crest of the hill . . . was strengthened by rifle trenches and occupied by infantry and artillery. In addition to this the plain was enfiladed by batteries on the other side of the Chickahominy. I was, in fact, in the position from which the enemy wished us to attack him."

The batteries of which Longstreet complained were part of McClellan's train of heavy siege guns on the south side of the river. As Longstreet's troops advanced across the plain, these 20- and 30-pound Parrotts, 32-pound howitzers, and 4½-inch Rodmans opened with telling effect, tearing holes in the advancing lines. But the lines closed up and the gray-clad infantry charged on, down the steep bank and up to the creek, before the murderous fire of artillery and musketry from the surrounding slopes forced a bloody withdrawal.

Meanwhile, Jackson's force, which had the longest march in order to reach Old Cold Harbor on Lee's extreme left, had finally gotten into position. Jackson had again been delayed by "the enemy having obstructed the road . . . and adopted the additional precaution to delay my march by defending the obstructions with sharpshooters. . . ." This threw him in rear of D. H. Hill's division, which reached Cold Harbor first and took position to the left of the road, waiting for Jackson. Ewell's force, under Jackson, was also late, having taken the wrong road, and in the process of reversing itself to get back on the proper route, so obstructed the road with wagons and ambulances that most of Jackson's artillery was not in position until the decisive phase of the battle was over. Only four batteries of about thirty guns were actually engaged and, according to Colonel Crutchfield, Jackson's chief of artillery, "among then were not enough guns of a suitable character to engage the enemy's guns. . . ."

Jackson put Ewell on Hill's right, then his own division and Whiting's division, connecting with A. P. Hill's left, and waited for Longstreet and A. P. Hill to drive the Federals across his front, according to Lee's battle plan. It soon became apparent, however, that the plan was not working, and realizing from the sound of the guns that Lee had run into trouble on the extreme right, Jackson ordered an attack, with D. H. Hill leading off.

With this new pressure mounting on his right, Porter now threw in his reserves to strengthen his rapidly thinning lines. McCall's division of Pennsylvanians, consisting of Meade's, Seymour's, and Reynolds's brigades, was put in on Morell's right and center to support Martindale and Griffin, who had borne the brunt of A. P. Hill's attacks. When the reinforcements Porter had been requesting all day, Slocum's division of Franklin's corps, finally arrived about 4 P.M., Taylor's and Newton's brigades filled the gap between Morell and Sykes, while Bartlett's brigade was sent to Sykes's right, where the Regulars were being pressed hard by D. H. Hill.

With Jackson in position and attacking, Lee now ordered a full-scale assault all along the line. Again A. P. Hill and Longstreet threw their troops forward, many of them passing over their own dead and wounded. As they swung out in open lines across the fields, the Federal batteries once more erupted violently. The ground seemed to shake and reel with the shock as the hot guns roared out their bloody message. It was one continuous roll like thunder, crashing and reverberating.

Across the fields and into the woods they charged, the battle lines broken into fragments by the march through the trees. Then the Federal line went into action with a crackling roar, as if it exploded. Yellow sheets of flame flashed from end to end, then disappeared in a heavy cloud of smoke. The noise roared to a crescendo that left the men dazed and confused. One veteran remembered, "The noise of the musketry was not rattling, as ordinarily, but one intense metallic din."

All along the line the battle ebbed and flowed, the issue in doubt. The Eleventh Pennsylvania and the Fourth New Jersey, finding themselves surrounded and cut off by Jackson's men, were forced to surrender in a body. In Morell's front, the Fifth Alabama and the First Tennessee lost their colors to the Second Maine and the Twenty-third New York in a series of vicious hand-to-hand engagements in which bayonets and clubbed muskets were freely used. Then the Sixteenth New York and the

Twentieth North Carolina tangled in what amounted to a personal war of their own over a battery supporting Sykes's division. In a daring charge the Southerners had driven the Federals back and captured the guns, only to have the New Yorkers recapture them ten minutes later in a reckless countercharge. In the process many of the New Yorkers lost their gay straw hats which their colonel's wife, Mrs. Howland, had recently sent them. The bright yellow hats with black ribbons and gilt letters presented a strange sight on the field between the dead and the wounded.

But Porter's line held. General Seymour reported: "Regiment after regiment advanced, relieved regiments in front, in turn withstood, checked, repelled, or drove the enemy, and retired, their ammunition being exhausted, to breathe a few moments, to fill their cartridge boxes, again to return to the contested woods. At times parts of the line would be driven from its ground, but only to receive aid and to drive the enemy in his turn. The woods were strewn with the heroic dead of both sides, and multitudes of wounded and dying painfully sought every hollow affording even momentary shelter from the incessant and pitiless fire."

By now A. P. Hill's division was almost completely demoralized. Some of the regiments had lost all their field-grade officers. In the smoke and confusion the men could not be rallied as they clung to their places in the woods behind the protection of the trees, or lay in the fields, or broke and ran for the rear. This, in effect, left a gap almost a mile wide in Lee's line through which an aggressive enemy could have driven to cut the Army of Northern Virginia in two. But McClellan not only was not aggressive, he wasn't even on the field, and Porter had no fresh troops to throw into the gap. Even if he had, it would not have done any good as he had orders not to pursue the enemy under any circumstances. With the troops he had, of course, it was unthinkable.

Hill's assaults had not been completely in vain, however. Morell's line had been thinned out, particularly in Martindale's brigade. Ammunition was running low and the men were exhausted. Many of the muskets were fouled from the heavy and continuous firing and were no longer usable. Another concentrated attack and part of the line might give way.

But time was running out on the Confederates. It was now after six o'clock and the shadows were lengthening. Lee, believing the situation was still critical, determined to make one more desperate attempt to break Porter's line. Realizing the condition of Hill's troops, he ordered Whiting's division of Jackson's command to replace Hill on Longstreet's left, and then ordered an all-out assault in an attempt to avert what he believed could still be a disaster for the Confederacy.

Forming for the attack in rear of Hill's shattered forces, Whiting's division became separated. In the confusion of the advance, which in some places was through and over remnants of various demoralized regiments, Hood inadvertently led two regiments of his Texas brigade, the Fourth Texas and Eighteenth Georgia, to the rear and right of Whiting's other brigade, commanded by Law, thus coming into line with Law on his left and Pickett's brigade, of Longstreet's division, on his right. His other troops, the First and Fifth Texas and the Hampton Legion, went in on Law's left, where the entire brigade was supposed to be. This was one of those "accidents" of battle which proved most fortunate for Lee. Without Hood's two regiments there would have been an interval between Law's and Pickett's brigades, which, as it developed, proved to be opposite the weakest point in Morell's front.

Realizing the strength of the Federal position and the dangers inherent in allowing the men to halt the advance to reload and fire, Whiting rode along the line and ordered the charge to be made at the double-quick with fixed bayonets and without firing. As they moved out to the attack an ominous quiet seemed to settle momentarily over the area. With the Confederate artillery long since knocked out of action on that part of the field, and their muskets at trail arms, the men trotted silently across the open fields in the gathering dusk in perfect alignment. Then the false quiet was rudely shattered by the sudden roar of the Federal artillery. A storm of lead and iron tore through the long gray lines as they disappeared into the smoke-shrouded woods on the edge of the creek, leaving the fields behind them strewn with dead and wounded. Down the slope through the trees they went, where the Federal musketry fire came out to meet the charging wave in a futile attempt to stem it. Some of the gray shapes went down, but the rest went on, a fearsome band of determined men, faces covered with sweat and grime, eyes bloodshot from dust, lips black from biting cartridges, screaming the high-pitched yell, shrill and exultant, that ended in a hideous, spine-chilling screech. One Federal soldier declared emphatically, "I have never, since I was born, heard so fearful a noise as the rebel yell." Only men who were going to kill or be killed could yell like that.

Jumping and wading the creek, they started up the other side. Then, somewhere about the center of Morell's line, the Federals broke and ran when the Confederates came within ten paces of it. They swarmed up the slope, carrying their second line with them and streamed across the plateau towards the river and safety. Into the gap stormed the Fourth Texas and the Eighteenth Georgia, quickly followed by Pickett's Virginians. The gap widened as the Federal regiments on the left and right were forced to pull back in order to keep from being outflanked and surrounded. But most of them withdrew in perfect order, still fighting, with little panic except at the breakthrough point, where Whiting's division captured fourteen pieces of artillery. Most of Morell's men retreated across the bridges directly south of the Watt house, while Sykes's men withdrew towards Alexander's and Grapevine bridges. During the withdrawal French's and Meagher's brigades, of Sumner's corps, arrived to help cover the retreat but were not engaged.

Trying to exploit the breakthrough to the fullest extent, Longstreet and Whiting advanced across the plateau in an attempt to capture several reserve batteries posted in the lowlands south of the Watt house. Acting without orders, but under what seemed like justifiable circumstances to him, General Cooke, commanding the cavalry reserve, ordered the Fifth U.S. Cavalry to charge the advancing infantry to give the artillerists time to bring off the reserve batteries. Across the plateau they thundered, sabers waving in a solid column of squadrons. But several of the field batteries, trying to withdraw, broke the column and threw it into confusion, and the Confederate infantry, which had halted and partly re-formed to receive the charge, quickly emptied over

100 saddles with a solid volley. Unfortunately, those who escaped this fire retreated through the artillery they were trying to save, adding to the confusion and undoubtedly causing the loss of some of the guns.

In his official report of the battle Porter wrote a scathing indictment of Cooke's action, blaming the cavalry for the failure of the Fifth Corps to hold the field. "This charge," he stated, "executed in the face of a withering fire of infantry and in the midst of heavy cannonading, resulted, of course, in their being thrown into confusion, and the bewildered horses, regardless of the efforts of the riders, wheeled about, and dashing through the batteries, convinced the gunners that they were charged by the enemy. To this alone is to be attributed our failure to hold the battlefield and bring off all our guns and wounded."

To claim that the charge "alone" caused the breakthrough was, of course, ridiculous on the face of it, and it is difficult to find a plausible excuse for Porter's action in this particular incident. Morell, commanding the division which had first given way, admitted that the Confederates in the last charge about 6:30 P.M. came "in irresistible force, and throwing themselves chiefly against the center and left, swept us from the ground by overwhelming numbers and compelled us to retire. As we retired the artillery opened fire from the left and rear, but the pressure was so great that the troops could not be rallied except in small bodies to support it." Longstreet stated: "When the cavalry came upon us our lines were just thin enough for a splendid charge upon artillery, but too thin to venture against a formidable cavalry," and he admitted that Pickett's men were within musketry range of the reserve batteries when the cavalry halted their advance. Law, of Whiting's division, was even more emphatic. "Whatever may be said to the contrary," he wrote, "it is certain that the batteries, having no infantry supports, did not check our advance for a moment. The diversion by the cavalry, on the other hand, did delay their capture for the short period it took to repulse it, and gave time for the artillerists to save some of their guns."

It could be that Porter was still harboring resentment against Cooke for his lack of aggressiveness in pursuing Stuart on the latter's famous ride around the Union army. That had been embarrassing for McClellan, particularly the lurid accounts of it that appeared in northern newspapers, and Porter and McClellan were close personal friends. It also could be, of course, that Porter was deliberately using the incident of the cavalry charge to protect McClellan against possible criticism for not reinforcing the Fifth Corps before the breakthrough. After all, if the cavalry charge alone caused Porter to lose possession of the field, then additional troops obviously were not needed.

It is true, as McClellan later claimed, that none of the other corps commanders seemed willing to send additional reinforcements to Porter, but this is understandable when it is remembered that McClellan had consistently warned them that he expected a heavy attack on the south side of the Chickahominy and that their line of entrenchments was to be considered their battle line. It was ridiculous to tell a corps commander one minute that he was going to be attacked by overwhelming numbers, and expect him the next minute to willingly send half his force somewhere else. McClellan made no attempt whatsoever to discover if Lee had weakened his line south of the river in order to mount his attack on the north side, as any good field commander would have done. With this knowledge he could have decided whether to feign an attack on his side and then reinforce Porter, or mount a full-scale assault and force Lee to move some troops to the south side in order to protect Richmond. The *least* McClellan could have done was to feign an attack in an attempt to relieve the pressure on the Fifth Corps. Instead, it was Magruder who spent the day feeling the enemy in his front with strong picket action, probing for any weakness in the Federal line. One of these actions developed into a skirmish about 7 P.M. when Toombs's Georgia brigade rashly attacked the Federal position about Golding's and Garnett's farms. The attack was quickly repulsed by Hancock's brigade, of Franklin's corps, with the Georgians losing over 400 men. This was the only action on the south side of the Chickahominy on June 27; yet at 8 P.M. McClellan telegraphed the secretary of war: "Attacked by greatly superior numbers in all directions on this side." This, apparently, was his answer in the event someone in Washington might wonder why he did not reinforce Porter, or at least make a diversion in his behalf. It is also revealing to note that anytime McClellan was attacked or he himself attacked, which was seldom, it was always by or against "superior numbers."

The point is, of course, that McClellan was not even thinking in terms of fighting Lee's army or attacking Richmond; he was preoccupied with one thought only: changing his base to the James and protecting his wagon and artillery trains in the process. It would not have altered his plans or actions in the least if Porter had held possession of the field at Gaines's Mill. The Fifth Corps would have been withdrawn under cover of darkness regardless. As McClellan admitted, "To have done more, even though Porter's reverse had been prevented, would have had the still more disastrous result of imperiling the whole movement across the Peninsula."

Regardless of whether the charge of the cavalry had saved or lost guns, it had discouraged any further advance on the part of the Confederates. Not that much discouragement was needed. After the terrible battle the men were exhausted—thirsty, dirty, and hungry. Whiting's division had lost over 1,000 men in the last charge; the Fourth Texas had lost every field-grade officer and over 250 men. Wilcox's brigade, of Longstreet's division, suffered almost 600 casualties, while Pickett's Virginia brigade lost over 400, including Pickett himself, who was seriously wounded. A member of his staff later expressed the belief that this was the hardest fight the brigade was ever in, with the one exception of Gettysburg. A private in the Fourth Texas put it more succinctly in a letter to his wife. "I am satisfied not to make another such charge."

In Jackson's front, Sykes's Regulars had withdrawn slowly and in good order towards Grapevine Bridge. Weed's and Tidball's batteries, supported by the Fourth U.S. Infantry, held their positions on the Cold Harbor road and discouraged any attempt by the Confederates to advance. The arrival of French and Meagher rendered the position secure, and all these outfits stayed on the north side of the river until the following morning. General Reynolds, brigade commander in McCall's division destined to die at Gettysburg, wandered around lost in the woods all night and then surrendered to Jackson's men in the morning.

The battle was over. In a sense, both sides had achieved their immediate objectives. Porter had held until night; so McClellan could get his army safely started towards Harrison's Landing on the James. Lee had cleared the north side of the Chickahominy of all Federal forces, broken their supply line to White House, controlled strategic New Bridge, and had turned back the Federal advance on Richmond, at least for the time being.

But Lee had lost something too, although he did not know it yet. With most of his army on the north side of the river, he was not in a good position to thwart McClellan's next move. In effect, McClellan had outmaneuvered him by moving the Federal army to where it would be most difficult for Lee to strike it.

As darkness settled like a gently restraining hand over the frightening confusion on the field that night, a silver sliver of moon cast its pale light over the ghastly scene. While the weary men sank into an exhausted sleep, the soul-searing moans of the wounded and dying echoed through the stillness of the woods. Motionless forms covered the ground in grotesque positions, as if someone had carelessly heaved them from a wagon. The Army of Northern Virginia had suffered over 8,000 casualties, the Army of the Potomac almost 7,000; and all of the dead and most of the wounded of both armies were still on the field. A foreign officer in the Confederate service, riding over the area, declared: "In by-gone days I had been on many a battlefield in Italy and Hungary; but I confess I never witnessed so hideous a picture of human slaughter and horrible suffering."

All through the night stretcher-bearers, friends and relatives of missing men, worked tirelessly among the thousands of dead and wounded, the flickering flames from the candles and lanterns casting weird shadows among the dark, silent trees. A Texas soldier wrote home: "I never had a clear conception of the horrors of war until that night. . . . On going round on that battlefield with a candle searching for my friends I could hear on all sides the dreadful groans of the wounded and their heart piercing cries for water and assistance. . . . Oh the awful scene witnessed on the battlefield. May I never see any more such in life. . . . I assure you I am heartily sick of soldiering."

On the Federal side of the river there was much confusion and

After the Battle

also speculation as to the next move. Porter's exhausted troops streamed across the bridges and fords, hungry and thirsty, looking for some place to rest, other than the swamps along the river's edge, where the putrid odor of half-buried men and horses from the battle of Seven Pines, a month ago, was suffocating. Companies, regiments, and even brigades were inextricably mixed, with most of the officers too tired and confused to straighten them out before morning. One soldier recalled the scene vividly: "Wagon trains, ammunition trains, detached masses from brigades, stragglers from a hundred regiments, wounded men, some on improvised stretchers, some supported by comrades, blocked the ground about the approaches to the bridges. The curses of the mule drivers mingled with the short, sharp orders of the officers, and the pleadings and expostulations of the wounded."

At Dr. Trent's house, just south of Grapevine Bridge, McClellan called a meeting of his corps commanders that lasted until two o'clock in the morning. He informed them of his plan to change his base of operation, his reasons for it, and the method of execution. Many days of preparation had gone into those plans; nothing, so far as possible, was being left to chance. The herd of beef cattle had left White House early that morning and was well on the way to the James; under the protection of gunboats, 800,000 rations were waiting for the army when it reached that river; the supplies at Dispatch Station, on the north side of the Chickahominy, were being transferred to Savage Station on the south side; most of the other supplies were already on their way down the York; the roads the army would use had been scouted, the topographical engineers had done their work, and now McClellan gave each of his corps commanders a map with the routes and positions marked.

This still left two major problems: passage of White Oak Swamp, and the safety of the wagon train and reserve artillery. The first had been partially solved, it was believed, by building bridges across the Swamp, but Barnard was now ordered to build more if necessary for the swift passage of the wagons. After the crossing of the army these would, of course, be destroyed. Also, since June 25 200 men had been kept busy chopping down trees to block all fords and passages through the Swamp once the army had passed over. These obstructions, combined with the natural heavy growth of the area, would create an effective deterrent to pursuing infantry, particularly if the fords and passes were covered by artillery.

The responsibility for the safety of the wagon train across the Swamp was given to Keyes and the Fourth Corps. The escort selected for the reserve artillery was McCall's division of Pennsylvania Reserves. Porter's Fifth Corps would follow Keyes, and while the Fourth Corps was guarding the passages across the Swamp, Porter would take up a position about an area known as Glendale which covered the roads leading from Richmond to White Oak Swamp and Long Bridge. The other three corps would remain in position except that they would withdraw about one mile to an interior line of entrenchments, thus giving more protection to the area about Savage Station. They would hold these positions until dark of the twenty-ninth. The wagons would load to capacity at Savage Station and what could not be carried would be destroyed if possible.

Every possibility seemed to be anticipated, all the details worked out to a fine point. If the maps were satisfactory, if all the existing roads were used properly, and if the commanding general stayed on the field and kept control with intelligent orders at critical times and places, the success of the movement seemed assured. McClellan believed that Lee would not expect him to make this move to the James, and this would result in the Confederate commander's hesitating to press the pursuit until he knew definitely what McClellan intended to do.

And somehow, in the midst of all these complicated logistical problems, the Young Napoleon still found time to send a long dispatch to the Secretary of War. It is one of the most amazing messages in military history, and must be quoted in its entirety for its significance to be fully appreciated.

June 28, 1862—12:20 A.M.

I now know the full history of the day. On this side of the river (the right bank) we repulsed several strong attacks. On the left bank our men did all that men could do, all that soldiers could accomplish, but they were overwhelmed by vastly superior numbers even after I brought my last reserves into action. The loss on both sides is terrible. I believe it will prove to be the most desperate battle of the war.

The sad remnants of my men behave as men. Those battalions who fought most bravely and suffered most are still in the best order. My regulars were superb, and I count upon what are left to turn another battle, in company with their gallant comrades of the volunteers. Had I 20,000 or even 10,000 fresh troops to use to-morrow I could take Richmond, but I have not a man in reserve, and shall be glad to cover my retreat and save the material and personnel of the army.

If we have lost the day we have yet preserved our honor, and no one need blush for the Army of the Potomac. I have lost this battle because my force was too small.

I again repeat that I am not responsible for this, and I say it with the earnestness of a general who feels in his heart the loss of every brave man who has been needlessly sacrificed today. I still hope to retrieve our fortunes, but to do this the Government must view the matter in the same earnest light that I do. You must send me very large re-enforcements, and send them at once. I shall draw back to this side of Chickahominy, and think I can withdraw all our material. Please understand that in this battle we have lost nothing but men, and those the best we have.

In addition to what I have already said, I only wish to say to the President that I think he is wrong in regarding me as ungenerous when I said that my force was too weak. I merely intimated a truth which today has been too plainly proved. If, at this instant, I could dispose of 10,000 fresh men, I could gain a victory tomorrow. I know that a few thousand more men would have changed this battle from a defeat to a victory. As it is, the Government must not and cannot hold me responsible for the result.

I feel too earnestly tonight. I have seen too many dead and wounded comrades to feel otherwise than that the Government has not sustained this army. If you do not do so now the game is lost.

If I save this army now, I tell you plainly that I owe no thanks to you or to any other persons in Washington.

You have done your best to sacrifice this army.

Geo. B. McClellan

To the military supervisor of telegraphs in Washington, E. S. Sanford, former president of the American Telegraph Company, the last two sentences sounded too close to treason; so on his own responsibility he deleted them from the copy of the telegram delivered to Stanton and the president. What effect this unauthorized act had on the history of the Civil War is impossible to determine because it naturally leads to historical "ifs," and historical "ifs" are similar to the variables in mathematics; they cannot be pinned down.

Even without those incriminating sentences, the dispatch is hysterical and completely unworthy of a general commanding an army in the field. It constituted definite grounds for dismissal from command, if not from the Army. And yet it was typical of so many of McClellan's dispatches—the same half-truths and distortion of facts, the same outright lies, all designed to obscure the true state of affairs and absolve McClellan from all blame and responsibility. He states baldly that he "repulsed several strong attacks" on his side of the river, when the truth was that the only report of any action was from one brigade, Hancock's, which easily repulsed Toombs's Georgia brigade in the skirmish just before dark and the end of the battle. But his statements about using his "last reserves" and the "sad remnants" of his men were much more serious. This implied, in no uncertain terms, that his whole army had been used in the battle of Gaines's Mill, when actually less than a third had been engaged. And his assertion that with 10,000 fresh troops he could take Richmond was ridiculous on the face of it, but, more important, it was also deliberate lie as he had no intention or plans for even attempting to take Richmond until after he changed his base. He had more than 75,000 troops who had not been in any battle since Seven Pines; yet he had the nerve to inform his government that "a few thousand more men would have changed this battle from a defeat to a victory." And his statement that he had lost the battle because "my force was too small" was another deliberate lie. He lost the battle because he did not use the force he had and because he refused to go on the offensive regardless of the circumstances and opportunities. McClellan's main objective in this dispatch seems to have been to paint the blackest picture possible so that if he succeeded in changing his base to the James it would appear to be a really brilliant movement made under terrific pressure from a numerically superior enemy.

The message, of course, even without the last two sentences, caused deep agitation in Washington. Secretary of State Seward left Washington immediately to confer in person with various state governors about raising new regiments, and to help arouse determination to continue the war. Stanton sent an urgent message to General Halleck at Corinth, Mississippi, to send 25,000 troops at once to McClellan. And Lincoln himself told his commander, "Save your army at all events. Will send re-enforcements as fast as we can." In other words, if it proved necessary, everyone would do everything possible to help McClellan and the army, as indeed they had been doing since the war began.

But McClellan answered: "It is impossible to tell where reenforcements ought to go, as I am yet unable to predict result of approaching battle." He was still refusing to inform Washington that he had made his plans to move to Harrison's Landing on the James, and that in fact the army was even then in the process of moving. And as for an "approaching battle," this was just more of McClellan's picture-painting for the record. But what was most confusing to the officials in Washington was that he was insisting he desperately needed more troops, but apparently didn't yet know where he needed them. It was difficult for anyone, other than McClellan, to see the logic in all this. Shortly after the message was sent communication was disrupted; so no further explanation was forthcoming.

Saturday, June 28, dawned clear and warm. On the Confederate side of the river confusion was rampant. Brigade and regimental commanders spent the early morning hours trying to bring order out of the chaos left over from the previous night. Many commands were hopelessly mixed and companies that had lost all their officers wandered around without direction, seeking orders. Battery commanders were trying desperately to find replacements for disabled cannons and dead horses. No one knew what orders the day might bring.

As the sun came up, yellow and hot, the bloody battlefield presented a ghastly scene. The paraphernalia of war littered the ground—coats, blankets, canteens, knapsacks, muskets, broken caissons, dead and wounded horses—and through it all the burial parties performing their grim task, ambulances carrying their gruesome loads into Richmond, the walking wounded hobbling along the roads, some with broken arms dangling at their sides, bloody heads, or faces burnt to a crisp by exploding powder. It was "awful and terrible beyond the power of human tongue to tell or pen to describe," wrote a young soldier from Georgia. "I thought that if all the women North and South could come upon the hills and valleys around Richmond and could see at once the many slain of their Fathers, husbands, sons, brothers, and lovers, that their weeping and wailing would be such, that it would wring tears from angelic eyes, and that there would be a ten fold greater clamor for peace among them than there ever was for war."

In the midst of all the confusion, Lee rode out over the field early that morning. Among other things, he was looking for his youngest son Robert, a private in the Rockbridge Artillery. He found him safe and sound, asleep under a caisson. But Lee's other problems could not be solved that quickly or easily.

Longstreet's advance guard pushed across the plateau and found the enemy gone and the bridges burned, but all the approaches to the river were well covered by Federal artillery. D. H. Hill advanced along the Cold Harbor road to Grapevine Bridge and encountered the same situation. McClellan had definitely abandoned the north side of the river, but the major question still remained unanswered: Where was he going?

There were several possibilities, as Lee saw it. McClellan could retreat back down the peninsula the way he had come, in which case he would have to recross the Chickahominy at some point lower down the river. Or, as Lee believed, after recrossing the river he still might attempt to fall back on White House to preserve his communications. In either event, Lee wanted to have his main body on the north side of the river where it now was. If, however, McClellan intended to stay behind his entrenchments until a new line of supply was established on the James River, then Lee would have to reunite his army on the south side of the Chickahominy, but in that case he would have plenty of time. There was also the possibility, of course, that McClellan would move his whole army to the James to protect this new base of operations, which would give the Confederates a wonderful opportunity to destroy the Federals en route, *if* Lee reunited his army in time. Until he knew definitely what McClellan was planning, however, Lee, for once in his career, was not willing to take the gamble that might have changed the whole course of the war. This unwillingness was undoubtedly based on his conviction that cautious McClellan would never attempt such a hazardous movement.

Consequently, early that morning Stuart's cavalry, supported by Ewell's division of Jackson's corps, was ordered to seize the

Richmond and York River Railroad and cut all communications between the Federal army and White House. Stuart advanced on Dispatch Station, driving off two companies of the Eighth Illinois Cavalry which retreated across Bottom's Bridge to the south side of the Chickahominy, burning it and the railroad trestle behind them. After destroying the station, cutting the telegraph line and tearing up some of the track, Stuart, without orders, determined "to push boldly down the White House road, resolved to find what force was in that direction and, if possible, rout it." Ewell decided to remain at Dispatch Station and await further orders.

Shortly before noon a huge cloud of dust rose up from across the river, indicating a large Federal column on the move somewhere. Then heavy explosions were heard in the distance, followed by thick clouds of black smoke swirling high in the air. Magazines and supplies were obviously being put to the torch. McClellan was definitely moving out from behind his entrenchments, but Lee was still not convinced that the Union forces were heading for the James. He knew that the abandonment of the railroad and the destruction of the bridges showed that they were not going to White House, but he insisted that from the position the Federal army occupied "the roads which led towards James River would also enable it to reach the lower bridges over the Chickahominy and retreat down the peninsula." Consequently, he believed "it was necessary that our troops should continue on the north side of the river, and until the intention of General McClellan was discovered it was deemed injudicious to change their disposition." It was not until late that night that Lee believed the "signs of a general movement were apparent, and no indications of his approach to the lower bridges of the Chickahominy having been discovered by the pickets in observation at those points, it became manifest that General McClellan was retreating to the James River." By then, of course, it was too late.

Immediately after McClellan's conference with the corps commanders the night of the battle, Keyes promptly started his Fourth Corps on its way to White Oak Swamp, with the exception of Naglee's brigade, of Peck's division, which was left behind to guard and then destroy the railroad and Bottom's bridges.

Keyes's orders stated he was to be across the Swamp before
daylight, but when he arrived at the crossing he found that for
some reason Hooker had previously destroyed the bridge and it
had not yet been repaired, and Barnard as yet had not built any
others. It was two hours after sunrise before the head of his leading division crossed the Swamp and seized the strong positions on
the other side to cover the passage of the wagon train and Porter's
Fifth Corps. If this was an indication of the coordination and
staff work to be expected during the movement, it was not a good
omen.

While the Fourth and Fifth corps, the wagon train, reserve
artillery, and herd of cattle proceeded across White Oak Swamp
on June 28, the other three corps held their positions as rear
guard. The only movement was by Franklin's Sixth Corps. Finding his line being heavily shelled by Confederate batteries near
Garnett's farm and on Gaines's hill across the river, he withdrew
a short distance and consolidated his corps about Golding's farm.
During the move two Georgia regiments again rashly attacked
the position at Golding's but were quickly driven off.

During the night of the twenty-eighth and early morning of
the twenty-ninth the three corps moved out, heading for White
Oak Swamp via Savage Station, with Franklin in the lead, fol-

Federals Crossing White Oak Swamp

White Oak Swamp

lowed by Sumner and Heintzelman. The wildest confusion prevailed. In the pitch blackness of the rainy night the men stumbled along the unfamiliar muddy roads, falling into ditches, tripping over the underbrush, floundering in the swamps, walking into bushes and limbs of trees. Men fell asleep marching; imagination played havoc, as mirages appeared before tired eyes; a clump of trees became a group of the enemy, a runaway horse a cavalry charge. Some regiments panicked, firing indiscriminately at shadows in the woods. Dead faces of lost buddies seemed to stare out between the trees. "It is no small tax upon one's endurance to remain marching all night," one veteran recalled. "During the day there is always something to attract the attention and amuse, but at night there is nothing."

Staff officers and messengers tried to work their way through the pandemonium along the roads, shouting orders and directions. Another veteran remembered the "ammunition wagons, hospital supplies, wagons loaded with food, horses and mules inextricably mixed, gun-carriages, blacksmith's forges, pontoons, all packed together," while some of the men, "tired and weary, were lying unblanketed, their feet to smouldering fires, dead with sleep, insensible to the heavy roll of artillery or the tramp of infantry."

But somehow, through all the chaos, progress was made. Slocum's division, of Franklin's corps, reached Savage Station about 5 A.M. on Sunday, June 29. Here a frightening scene of destruction awaited them, as huge piles of supplies and munitions were put to the torch. A surgeon in the Seventy-seventh New York remembered seeing "boxes of hard bread, hundreds of barrels of flour, rice, sugar, coffee, salt and pork thrown upon the burning piles," along with boxes of clothing and shoes. An officer in the Seventh Maine saw a "long line of whiskey barrels" being destroyed, but not quickly or efficiently enough to keep the resourceful among the stragglers from getting drunk. Large magazines of powder, cartridges, and shells exploded with a whooshing boom. A railroad train was filled with excess ordnance stores, the cars set on fire, and the whole shebang set in motion down the tracks towards the burned trestle to splash into the Chickahominy. Some of the shells exploded high in the smoke, cascading a metal spray over the general area, followed by the rattle of bursting cartridges in one great metallic roar.

In the midst of the smoke, noise, and confusion, McClellan appeared in person and ordered Slocum to continue on across White Oak Swamp, without waiting for the rest of the corps. Then McClellan packed up his headquarters and disappeared in the direction of the James River as the remainder of Franklin's corps and Sumner's advance troops put in an appearance.

On the other side of the river Lee finally issued his orders early that morning of the twenty-ninth. With the Federal army in motion for the James, his problem was to find the most effective way and best place to hit it. But he would have to plan pretty much in the dark. For one thing, he had no cavalry for reconnaissance.

After driving off the Federal patrol at Dispatch Station the day before, Stuart, without orders, had proceeded down the railroad towards White House. Encamping that night at Tunstall's Station, he reached White House on the morning of the twenty-ninth, in time to see the last gunboat just leaving, nine barges loaded with stores blazing fiercely, and "immense numbers of tents, wagons, cars in long trains loaded and five locomotives, a number of forges, quantities of every species of quartermaster's stores and property, making a total of many millions of dollars—all more or less destroyed."

But other things were not destroyed, such as the sutler's shops, and soon Stuart's troopers, who had been subsisting on a diet of salt meat and crackers, were regaling themselves with bottles of champagne and casks of beer, wine, and whiskey, along with "pickled oysters, eggs roasted in blocks of salt, canned beef and ham, French rolls, cakes and confectionery of all sorts," topped off with fine Havana cigars. Understandably, Stuart reported, "It took the remainder of Sunday to ration my command. . . ."

It is quite possible, of course, that if the cavalry had been available Lee would not have used it for reconnaissance on the south side of the river. Even while he was issuing orders to cross the Chickahominy, he requested Stuart to watch for any movement of the enemy back across the river. Apparently he still feared, at that late date, that McClellan might be heading down the peninsula. Also, he reported that "below the enemy's works the country was densely wooded and intersected by impassable swamps, at once concealing his movements and precluding reconnaissances except by regular roads, all of which were strongly guarded." Yet the fact remains that had Lee used Stuart's cavalry for a reconnaissance in force on the south side of the river the day before, that is, June 28, when the Federal movement to the James began, the pursuit could have been started earlier and undoubtedly would have been much more effective.

As it was, Lee had no idea how far the Federal army had gone by now, nor exactly where on the James River its ultimate destination was. His immediate problem, however, was to get all his divisions in motion by different roads at once, if possible. A look at the map showed him that probably his best chance to strike the Federal column would be below White Oak Swamp, on the hope that passage through the Swamp would delay it long enough to give his divisions time to get into position. Consequently, when he received word early that morning, the twenty-ninth, that the Federal entrenchments had been abandoned, he ordered A. P. Hill and Longstreet to cross the Chickahominy at New Bridge and move by the Darbytown road to the Long Bridge road, which ran south and east of White Oak Swamp. Magruder, already on the south side of the river on the Williamsburg road, was ordered in pursuit of the retreating Federals so as to hit their rear guard as they crossed the Swamp. Huger, also on the south side, was to take the Charles City road, which met the Long Bridge road at a place called Glendale, and hit the Federals in flank as they emerged from the Swamp onto the Long Bridge road. Jackson and D. H. Hill were directed to cross at Grapevine Bridge and move down the south side of the Chickahominy, which would put them also on the Federal rear, next to Magruder.

At first glance it might seem that it would have been better just to move Huger, on the Charles City road, over to the Darbytown road, and Magruder, on the Williamsburg road, over to the Charles City road, to let Longstreet and Hill, on the north side of the river, take the first road after crossing, which would be the Williamsburg road. But the critical elements to Lee now were speed and time, and Huger and Magruder were the only ones in position to apply pressure immediately on the Federal rear. Lee hoped that Magruder and Jackson, harassing McClellan's rear, combined with Huger hitting below the Swamp, would delay the movement long enough for Longstreet and Hill to get into position.

The strategy involved here was excellent, but again it was the time element that doomed Lee's hopes. The twenty-four hour delay in issuing his orders to cross the river was fatal. From that time on it was relatively simple for the Federal corps commanders to fight effective delaying actions to protect their withdrawal. The result was the Confederates never came close to striking at the middle of the enemy columns, as Lee had hoped; all they ever hit was the rear guard.

Shortly after sunrise on the twenty-ninth the last of the Union forces, Richardson's division of Sumner's corps, pulled out of the entrenchments around Fair Oaks and retreated toward Savage Station. The works were immediately occupied by the Second South Carolina, the leading regiment of Kershaw's brigade, Magruder's command. Pressing on, Kershaw about nine o'clock ran into Richardson's division drawn up in line of battle across Allen's farm, about two miles east of Fair Oaks, and started to attack. When Richardson opened up with three batteries, however, Kershaw withdrew to the shelter of some woods, and the action ceased about eleven o'clock. Richardson then proceeded to Savage Station unmolested, where Sumner put him into line.

The situation around Savage Station was now becoming confused. Sumner, being the senior officer on the field, took the liberty of ordering Heintzelman's and Franklin's corps into position when he received a report that the Confederates were crossing the Chickahominy to attack him. Heintzelman, however, decided to continue on across White Oak Swamp even though Sumner had decided to make a stand at Savage Station. In his report Heintzelman stated: "The whole open space near Savage's was crowded with troops—more than I supposed could be brought into action judiciously." He also realized that all the troops concentrated there could not cross the Swamp safely on

the few existing roads, bridges, and fords, in the event they had
to do it under pressure. Consequently, unable to find McClellan
and with no word from army headquarters, Heintzelman ordered
his artillery across the bridge at Brackett's Ford, the infantry
crossing at Fisher's and Jourdan's fords.

As it developed, Heintzelman was right. Sumner did not have
to use all the troops available, even after the Third Corps left. He
put Richardson's division in an open field north of the railroad
tracks in back of the station. Sedgwick's division held the center
in another open field south of the tracks, with its left resting on
the Williamsburg road. "Baldy" Smith's division, of Franklin's
corps, took position in the rear of Sedgwick and in the woods
south of the road. These were all the troops that were even upon
the line. By 3:30 P.M. the last of the wagons and reserve artillery
had left Savage Station and started across White Oak Swamp.

Early that morning Lee himself had crossed the river and rode
down Nine Mile Road. Here Magruder joined him, and Lee
explained to him what he wanted done. Despite this personal
conference, however, Magruder was apparently confused. He was

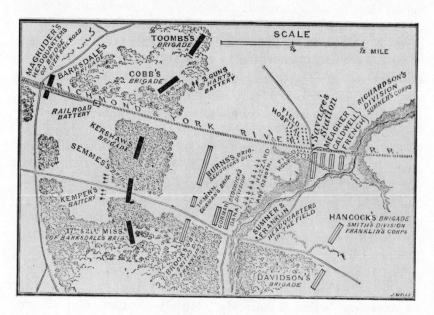

Battle of Savage Station

under the impression that Huger was supposed to be advancing on the Williamsburg road, rather than the Charles City road, and that he was to act only in concert with Huger and Jackson. The result was he moved very slowly, ordering his brigade commanders to advance "cautiously" and not to engage the enemy until ordered to do so. When he finally reached the vicinity of Savage Station and his brigade commanders reported the enemy in force in their fronts, Magruder decided to halt and wait for Jackson's arrival. Then, insisting he was about to be attacked, he sent an urgent request to Lee for support. Lee ordered two of Huger's brigades from the Charles City road to his support, but by the time they arrived it was apparent that no attack was forthcoming, that all Magruder had in his front was the Federal rear guard; so they were sent back and Magruder was again ordered to attack.

It was now almost five o'clock. Magruder had Semmes's brigade across the Williamsburg road, with Kershaw on his left in a belt of woods extending to the tracks and fronting on an open field. Cobb's and Toombs's brigades were north of the railroad, with Barksdale's in reserve near the railroad bridge where Magruder had his headquarters. On the tracks was the railroad battery that Lee had previously requested the Confederate Navy to build, with the idea of stopping the flow of McClellan's supplies along that line. It was a banded and rifled 32-pounder gun, mounted on a railroad flatcar and protected in front by a sloping metal sheet. Magruder moved it forward and used it to open his attack, this being the first known use of railroad artillery in combat.

The mobile cannon proved relatively ineffective, however, being vulnerable to sharpshooters on both sides, and when the Seventy-second Pennsylvania, of Burns's brigade, Sedwick's division, was used to rake it with fire, it was quickly withdrawn. Kershaw and Semmes then tried to advance but ran into a devastating blast from Sedgwick's division, supported by Pettit's, Hazard's, and Osborn's batteries, forcing a halt. When Brooks's brigade, of Smith's division, Franklin's corps, opened fire on Semmes from the woods south of the Williamsburg road, Magruder detached two regiments from Barksdale's brigade, the Seventeenth and Twenty-first Mississippi, and sent them to cover the right flank. These were the only forces engaged in this affair, generally referred to as the "battle" of Savage Station. Magruder failed to get Toombs's, Anderson's, or Cobb's brigades into action, with the result that Richardson's division on Sumner's right flank was not engaged at all, and only part of one brigade of Franklin's corps was involved.

Lee was not happy with the results of the day's actions and apparently held Magruder primarily responsible. "I regret much that you have made so little progress today in the pursuit of the enemy," he informed Magruder that night. It was obvious to Lee his plan was not working and it looked now as if McClellan might escape him entirely. With Magruder's dilatory tactics and lack of aggressive action, Longstreet and A. P. Hill might not be able to come up in time to inflict any damage on the Federals. But why Lee blamed only Magruder, and not Jackson and Huger, is difficult to understand.

Actually, there was little else Magruder could have done. To be sure, he was slow in getting his division in motion and he bungled the attack by not using all his available forces. Also, he

Federal Retreat from Savage Station

should not have delayed the attack to await Jackson's arrival as his orders were to press the enemy vigorously regardless of Jackson's position. If Lee had wanted him to wait for Jackson, he would have ordered him to do so. But Magruder was heavily outnumbered and the Federals had some strong redoubts across the Williamsburg road. Lee did not realize that Magruder was facing almost two Federal corps, even though less than half of that force was engaged. Even if Magruder had attacked earlier and with all his force, the result probably would have been the same.

Huger was also cautious in his advance, however, and he was not particularly aggressive, although sending two brigades to Magruder did complicate things somewhat. Huger himself led Ransom's brigade back to Seven Pines, with Wright's following, while Mahone and Armistead continued on down the Charles City road. The day was intensely hot, and this marching and countermarching was not conducive to speed or aggressiveness. By the time Huger finally got his division together again it was late afternoon, and the leading brigade, Mahone's, had only reached Brightwell's house, just west of Fisher's and Jourdan's fords, where Heintzelman's infantry rear guard was just then crossing. When Huger's flankers were fired upon by the Federal skirmishers, he halted the column and deployed his forces to reconnoiter the area. Like Magruder, he now believed he was being attacked; so he ordered up a battery and the Forty-fourth Alabama to guard the road from Jourdan's Ford and then went into bivouac for the night, while the Federal infantry continued on its way. He was only six miles from where he had started that morning. It would seem then that Huger was as much at fault as Magruder for the poor showing of the day.

Jackson, of course, never did arrive in time to participate in the action, not reaching Savage Station until early the next morning. Lee reported he "was delayed by the necessity of reconstructing Grapevine bridge." Jackson certainly didn't show any particular alacrity in repairing the bridge, as he reported that he had started work on it at 11 P.M. the night of the twenty-eighth when the Federal artillery withdrew. As twelve hours had been sufficient time for New Bridge to be repaired for the passage of both infantry and artillery, it does seem as if Jackson should have been ready to advance by noon on the twenty-ninth. There was nothing specific in Jackson's orders about the need to hurry, but it was certainly evident to every divisional commander that the Federal army was getting away and that only prompt and cooperative action on the part of all the commanders could prevent its escape. But when Magruder sent a message asking when Jackson would cross and come to his support, Jackson curtly replied that he could not cooperate with him as he had "other important duty to perform." It is true, of course, that Magruder was supposed to attack the Federal rear guard when he caught up with it, regardless of Jackson's position, but the mere fact of Jackson's command crossing the river and threatening Sumner's right flank at Savage Station would have been cooperation in itself. It probably would not have changed the course of the battle, however, as Richardson's division was in position to hold up any Confederate advance long enough for a safe withdrawal, and Franklin's corps was also available if needed.

When Lee was informed of Jackson's reply to Magruder, he quickly countermanded it by ordering Jackson to join Magruder at once, but by then, of course, it didn't make any difference. It was becoming increasingly apparent that Lee's staff work left much to be desired. Either Jackson, Huger, and Magruder did not understand Lee's plan, or they were seemingly incapable of carrying it out effectively. It is significant that after the affair at Savage Station Lee ordered Magruder to march to the Darbytown road and follow Longstreet. This left only Jackson, working alone, covering the Federal rear. It is, of course, impossible to determine exactly why Lee did this, but one thing is certain: it was a mistake. It may be that Lee realized Jackson and Magruder could not work together, and after Magruder's poor showing at Savage Station he probably did not want him in a responsible and important position in any forthcoming battle. And yet, it is interesting to speculate on what might have happened if Magruder had been with Jackson at White Oak Swamp the next day.

The only bright spot in Lee's whole day was when he was notified that General Holmes and 6,000 troops had crossed the

James River from the south side, where they had been holding Fort Darling on Drewry's Bluff, and the War Department had sent them down the New Market road to try to get between McClellan and the James. These reinforcements almost compensated for the Confederate losses at Gaines's Mill.

Conclusion
of the Seven Days:
Glendale and Malvern Hill

Old General Sumner was happy with the day's results. He apparently believed he had fought and won a major battle, instead of a small affair in which little more than two Confederate brigades had been involved. He wanted to stay there and fight, and at first refused to let Franklin move his corps out, telling him, "I never leave a victorious field." But then a direct order from McClellan to withdraw across White Oak Swamp during the night changed his mind.

To many of the men in the Army of the Potomac, however, it was a particularly sad day. McClellan ordered that all of the sick and wounded who could not march be left behind for lack of transportation. A large field hospital had been set up just north of the railroad tracks at Savage Station, and more than 2,500 sick and wounded men were left there to be captured. It was almost as

142

hard on the men who had to leave as it was on those left behind. As one veteran wrote: "Brave men, who have unfalteringly approached belching cannon, driven away those who served them at the point of the bayonet, and laid their hands on the hot breech as proof of capture, have trembled with grief and turned away speechless from the pleading countenances of those whom they have stood beside in battle, and now must leave to fall into the hands of the enemy."

For those who marched away it meant another night of stumbling through the dark and the rain and the mud, halting and marching, marching and halting, and always the nerve-wracking false alarms. "Wet clothes, shoes and blankets," one soldier wrote disgustedly. "Wet ground to sleep on, mud to wade through, swollen creeks to ford, muddy springs to drink from." And in the morning, wrote another veteran, when they reached their assigned position, "we lay down in our blankets, bedraggled, wet, and tired, chewing hard-tack and the cud of reflection, the tenor of which was 'Why did we come for a soldier?' "

But they all got safely through White Oak Swamp that night. Franklin went first, followed by Sumner, with Richardson's division acting as rear guard. Richardson took up his line of march at one o'clock in the morning and about 10 A.M., his division safely across, he burned the bridge at the main crossing. He was not pursued or pressured from the rear at any time. Then he took up a position on the heights west of the road, with Smith's division, of Franklin's corps, east of the road, to guard the crossing.

At just about the same time McClellan held a conference with three of his corps commanders—Sumner, Heintzelman, and Franklin—at Glendale, the junction of the Charles City, Quaker, and Long Bridge roads. Porter's and Keyes's corps were already at Malvern Hill, about three miles south of Glendale, as was most of the reserve artillery and the wagon train. After instructing them about the disposition of the troops at Glendale and sending Franklin back to White Oak Swamp to take personal charge of that defense, McClellan and his staff left for the James River and the gunboats. With no one actually in command, the success of any action that might take place about Glendale would be

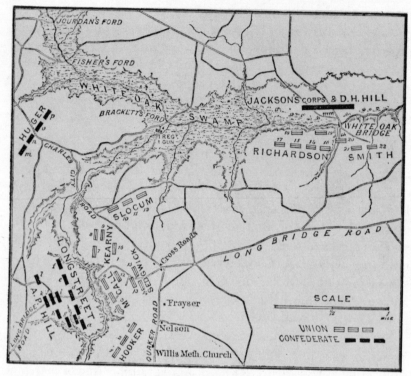

Battle of Glendale

strictly dependent upon cooperation and staff work among the three corps commanders. And with their divisions and brigades inextricably mixed, it would require good judgment and quick action on the part of divisional and brigade commanders also.

Slocum's division, of Franklin's corps, was posted by McClellan north of the Charles City road in front of the junction of the road from Brackett's Ford, and about one mile west of the crossroads at Glendale. Heintzelman had already burned the bridge at the ford and effectively blocked the road from there as well as the Charles City road. Slocum was facing northwest to cover any advance that Huger might attempt down the Charles City road, but he also took the precaution to send one 12-pound howitzer and one regiment to guard the ford. Heintzelman then put Kearny's division on Slocum's left, facing southwest and extending almost to the Long Bridge road. Beyond this was supposed to be

Hooker's position, but Heintzelman found to his dismay that McClellan had already put McCall's division there, after McCall had safely escorted the reserve artillery to that point and been relieved of its responsibility as it continued on to Malvern Hill. So Hooker was put in line on McCall's left, parallel to the Quaker road and extending beyond Willis Church. McClellan sent word back that Sedgwick's division was on the Quaker road and could be used as a reserve; so Sumner ordered it up and put it in rear of McCall's division.

Despite the complications and confusion all were in position shortly after noon, with all the roads well protected and guarded. There were two weak spots in the line, however, that could mean trouble, depending, of course, on where the Confederates put the most pressure. Slocum's and McCall's divisions had both lost over 2,000 men each in the past few days. If either one gave way the situation could become rather ticklish, as McCall had more or less of an independent command, not being attached to any corps at that point. And while Slocum belonged to Franklin's corps, Franklin himself was back at White Oak Swamp with his other division, Smith's and Richardson's division of Sumner's corps, and Sumner was at Glendale with Sedgwick's division. Who was responsible for what and to whom? A command setup like that, with not even a staff officer from army headquarters on the field, was an open invitation to disaster.

Although Grapevine Bridge had finally been repaired the night of the twenty-ninth, Jackson did not succeed in crossing all his command until the following morning and did not reach White Oak Swamp in full force until noon, two hours after the Federals had burned the bridge. Under cover of the heavily wooded area Jackson put twenty-six guns from Hill's division and five from Whiting's on a bluff to the right of the road, and about two o'clock opened with a terrifying roar on Richardson's division on the other side of the Swamp. The fire was so sudden and unexpected that some of the Federal teamsters were caught at the edge of the Swamp watering the mules. The bursting shells panicked the animals, and, as one soldier remembered, they "ran through Meagher's brigade and disabled more men than were injured by the enemy's artillery." Then Richardson's and Smith's artillery boomed their answer to the challenge, and the duel continued the rest of the day with neither side inflicting any serious damage on the other. Some of Jackson's cavalry succeeded in crossing a ford lower down the creek but were quickly driven back, and although the cavalry commander reported the crossing as practical for infantry, Jackson made no attempt to cross.

Meanwhile, Longstreet and A. P. Hill, who had marched about fourteen miles over unobstructed roads on the twenty-ninth and encamped that night at the junction of the Darbytown and Long Bridge roads, advanced down the Long Bridge road and ran into McCall's pickets about noon. After driving them in and discovering the Federals were there in position and strength, Longstreet halted to put his division in line for a fight. Pryor's, Featherstone's, and Wilcox's brigades went to the left of the road, opposite McCall's right and Kearny's left, and Pickett's, Anderson's, and Kemper's brigades to the right, opposite McCall's left and Hooker's right. Branch's brigade was ordered up to support Kemper on the right, but the rest of Hill's division was held in the rear in reserve until late in the battle. Longstreet then waited for a signal from Huger, supposed to be coming down the Charles City road, to begin the attack. And here he was joined by Lee and Jefferson Davis, on the field as usual.

About this time Lee learned that the force under Holmes on the New Market road below Malvern Hill had been stopped by a devastating artillery fire from the hill and the gunboats on the James. Earlier, Lee had observed what he believed to be indications of confusion in the Federal retreat at that point, and had ordered Holmes to advance. What Lee had actually seen, however, was merely the last of the wagons and the reserve artillery disappearing over Malvern Hill under the protection of Porter's Fifth Corps. And when Holmes tried to advance, Porter's massed guns on the hill opened on him; and Warren's brigade, of Sykes's division, was sent to block his advance on the road. Lee then ordered Magruder, who was coming down the Darbytown road, to Holmes's support, but Magruder floundered around on different roads until it was dark; so Holmes withdrew.

When the sound of Jackson's artillery at White Oak Swamp reached Longstreet sometime after two o'clock, he thought it was

Huger advancing on the Charles City road and hitting the Federal right flank. Immediately he ordered his guns to open up and the division to attack. Then complete confusion seemed to take over. The brigade commanders were completely unfamiliar with the ground over which they were ordered to advance. In the swamps, woods, and ravines alignments were broken and reformed again and again, regiments lost contact with each other on the flanks, and the advance degenerated into a series of partial attacks at different times and places. The left of the line started the attack about 4 P.M., but it was after 5 P.M. before the regiments on the right advanced. There was little coordination among the brigades, and the staff work at divisional headquarters left much to be desired. Longstreet stated in his report: "Owing to the nature of the ground that concert of action so essential to complete success could not obtain, particularly attacking such odds against us and in position."

But the fighting, nevertheless, was vicious, most of it being close hand-to-hand regimental actions, where clubbed muskets and bayonets were freely used. Federal batteries, which McCall had placed in front of his infantry, were taken and retaken and then taken again. The attack on the left hit Meade's brigade and Reynolds's old brigade on McCall's right and developed into an isolated fight over possession of Randol's battery of 12-pound Napoleons. One section of the battery was captured by the Eleventh Alabama, of Wilcox's brigade, when the Fourth Pennsylvania gave way under the pressure. The Alabamans had suffered fearful losses, however, and when Lieutenant Randol managed to rally a few companies of the Pennsylvanians, he quickly recaptured his guns, only to have the Fifty-fifth and Sixtieth Virginia, of Field's brigade, Hill's division, come up and retake them. The Ninth and Tenth Alabama captured another section of the ill-fated battery south of the road. Randol lost six guns altogether before the bloody day closed. General Meade was seriously wounded and Colonel Simmons, in temporary command of Reynolds's brigade, was killed. But the line held.

The attack on the right fell on Seymour's brigade, on McCall's left and Hooker's right, and for a time it appeared as if the Confederates might break through. The Twelfth Pennsylvania, on Seymour's left, became separated and confused, and when Kemper's brigade hit them they broke. Two German batteries of four 20-pound Parrotts each, from McCall's division of Porter's corps, under Captains Diederich and Knieriem, also limbered up and withdrew at the first volley. Behind them was the Fourth Pennsylvania Cavalry, dismounted and lying on the ground to escape the hail of lead and iron, and before most of them could mount the batteries and the infantry ran through them, scattering their horses. This confusion, and what looked like panic with the runaway horses, was what caused Hooker to claim in his report that McCall's division was overrun. McCall and Seymour, however, quickly brought the Fifth and Tenth Pennsylvania and part of the "Bucktails" into line to stem the advance. McCall was now desperately looking for reinforcements. Fortunately the confused mass of retreating men and horses flowed right by the Frayser house on the Quaker road where Sumner had his headquarters, and Sumner, thinking the line was broken, quickly sent two brigades to McCall's support. Earlier, Franklin had called for help when he believed he was being attacked at Brackett's Ford, and Sumner had sent him these two brigades. When it proved to be a false alarm Franklin immediately returned them, and they arrived back just in time to support McCall. Then with the help of one of Hooker's brigades, the situation was stabilized.

Slocum, on the Federal right, had not been engaged all day, except for some artillery and sharpshooting action. Huger had advanced less than a mile, his explanation being: "After passing Fisher's house we found the road obstructed by trees felled all across it. General Mahone found it best to cut a road around the obstructions. For such work we were deficient in tools. The column was delayed while the work was going on, and it was evening before we got through and drove off the workmen, who were still cutting down other trees." In this "battle of the axes" why Mahone found it best to do something for which he wasn't equipped Huger didn't bother to explain. Nor did he explain why it took him all day to drive off the "workmen." About noon Mahone had very cautiously advanced down the road to Brackett's Ford, but when he ran into the one regiment and one gun there, he halted to "reconnoiter." This was when Franklin had rushed up two brigades, thinking it might be a spirited attack, and Slocum sent up a battery of the Fourth U.S. Artillery to support the lone regiment. The battery shelled the woods in front for about half an hour and then withdrew. By the time the two brigades reached the ford Mahone had withdrawn to the Charles City road. In his report of the affair Mahone rather naively stated: "The loss of the brigade in this engagement was serious. . . . The 41st Virginia, which suffered more severely than any other regiment . . . lost in killed 1 officer and 17 privates and in wounded 18 privates."

In McCall's front, however, the fighting continued until dark. With two brigade commanders and most of his personal staff out of action, McCall was kept busy trying to keep control of his division and at the same time find reinforcements. Kearny eventually sent him two regiments, and Heintzelman persuaded Slocum to send Taylor's New Jersey brigade over to support the center of the Federal line. Just as darkness fell McCall rode forward on the Long Bridge road to ascertain the position of the Fourth Pennsylvania, supposed to be in that area, and rode right into the Forty-seventh Virginia and was taken prisoner. The battle was over.

As far as Lee was concerned, of course, it was another military zero similar to Beaver Dam. Nothing had been accomplished. But the possibilities had looked good. With three columns converging on the moving Federal army, Jackson in the rear, Huger on the flank, and Longstreet near the front, it had seemed as if something should have been accomplished. The trouble was the tactics required for the successful completion of this strategy were much too complicated for this early period of the war. To begin with, Lee had been twenty-four hours late putting his divisions in motion, which further complicated things from the start. The country through which they were maneuvering, heavily wooded with numerous streams, swamps, ravines, gullies, and narrow, twisting country roads, combined with the lack of adequate maps, gave the advantage to the pursued, not the pursuers. The ignorance of the topography led the Confederates to underestimate the effectiveness of blocking roads and fords and destroying bridges. Offsetting these disadvantages required sound tactics, close cooperation between the divisional commanders involved, and excellent staff work at army headquarters. Lee had none of these.

If Huger and Jackson, for example, could have cooperated on both sides of White Oak Swamp at Brackett's Ford, it might have made a big difference in the outcome of this particular battle. Also, if Lee had sent Magruder, who had wasted the whole day in a senseless march from Savage Station to the Darbytown road, from Savage Station down the road to Brackett's Ford on the north side of the Swamp, with Jackson on his left at the main crossing and Huger on his right on the south side of the Swamp at the ford, and *if* they had acted in concert under directions from Lee's headquarters and attacked aggressively at the same time, the Federal army could have been in serious trouble.

Jackson's complete inertia, of course, will probably always remain a mystery. The main criticism is not that he didn't force a crossing at the Swamp, but that he didn't even try. It would not have been easy in any event, and without the active cooperation of Huger or some other division, probably impossible. After all, there were two good divisions with massed artillery under Franklin's command contesting the crossing, and the roads and fords had been effectively blocked. The weak point, of course, was Brackett's Ford, just a mile above Jackson's position at White Oak Bridge, but he didn't even make a reconnaissance in that direction. Nor did any staff officer come from Lee's headquarters to find out what the trouble was or to urge an immediate advance. And neither Huger nor Jackson thought it necessary to inform the general commanding of their situation and position at any time. In his report Jackson stated: "A heavy cannonading in front announced the engagement of General Longstreet at Frazier's farm and made me eager to press forward; but the marshy character of the soil, the destruction of the bridge over the marsh and creek, and the strong position of the enemy for defending the passage prevented my advancing until the following morning."

Several theories have been advanced to explain Jackson's failure. Dabney, in his biography of Jackson, states: "The temporary eclipse of Jackson's genius was probably to be explained by physical causes." But D. H. Hill, Jackson's brother-in-law, wrote after the war: "I think that an important factor in this inaction was Jackson's pity for his own corps, worn out by long and exhausting marches, and reduced in numbers by its numerous sanguinary battles. He thought that the garrisons of Richmond ought now to bear the brunt of the fighting." The truth probably lies somewhere in between these two theories.

For the Federals it had been a victory, in a sense, as a serious threat to their rear had been thwarted and the most dangerous obstacle in their march had been overcome successfully. It probably would not have been disastrous, however, even if part of the line had been overwhelmed. The reserve artillery and almost all of the wagon train was already safely behind Malvern Hill when the battle commenced, and Porter had his corps and Keyes's in position on the hill to defend it; the rest of the army could have rallied behind the hill. McClellan can hardly be credited with the victory, however, as he wasn't even on the field, although he had placed some of the divisions earlier. McCall reported: "Of the four divisions that day engaged, each maneuvered and fought independently." And yet Heintzelman and Sumner deserve some of the credit, for even though neither of them was actually in command on the field, they both acted promptly and judiciously to get reinforcements when needed to various sectors of the line, a delicate problem considering the command setup under which they were working. And towards the close of the battle Franklin had cooperated by sending Caldwell's and Meagher's brigades of Richardson's division when Sumner requested them.

Sumner again apparently believed they had won a great battle rather than a successful rearguard action, and refused to leave the field without a direct order from the commanding general. But when Franklin and Heintzelman decided to retire without orders, Sumner was forced to follow. Franklin moved out first and fortunately found a seldom used road about two miles east of the Quaker road that he could use, thus easing the congestion on the latter road. Heintzelman then moved down the Quaker road, followed by Sumner. All were in position at Malvern Hill shortly after daybreak.

The position selected by Porter and Barnard for the last stand before reaching the James was another naturally strong one. On the crest of a hill, it was flanked on either side by creeks in deep ravines less than a mile apart, and across this narrow front Porter placed his batteries with the guns almost hub to hub. He had all of the reserve artillery to call on if needed. In front the ground was open, sloping down to woods, marshes, swamps, and creeks, through which the Confederate forces would have to form for attack within range of the massed Federal artillery on the hill. The Quaker road ran directly south through the center of the position.

Porter put Sykes's division on the left facing due west and covering all the roads from Richmond near the James River. Then came Morell's division on Sykes's right, curving around the Crew house and facing generally west and north, and extending to the Quaker road. McClellan, on the field temporarily early in the morning, placed Couch's division of Keyes's corps on Morell's right, east of the Quaker road, facing north and east, and extending almost to the creek guarding that flank. Behind him the three corps of Heintzelman, Franklin, and Sumner were held in reserve, more or less, although also charged with guarding the right rear of the position. The rest of Keyes's corps and McCall's weary, cut-up division, now under Seymour, were farther back at the Malvern House.

By noon all were in position. The sun was a red ball of flame in a solid wall of blue, as the heat rose from the marshy ground in steaming waves. And then, as at Gaines's Mill, there came a sudden silence. The men lay quiet in the sultry air, gazing expectantly toward the silent trees in their front, wondering when the gray shapes would come. These intense moments before a battle passed agonizingly slow. "Never did I know before how hard it is to fight," wrote one soldier. "It is not fear, but uncertainty that so strains the nerves and makes men live days in every moment."

They would have several more hours to wait, however, before the Confederates arrived. Nothing seemed to have gone right for Lee that day. Huger, thinking the Charles City road was still blocked, at 3 A.M. sent Armistead's and Wright's brigades on another road to the west which crossed the Long Bridge road and then led to the Malvern Hill area, west of the Quaker road.

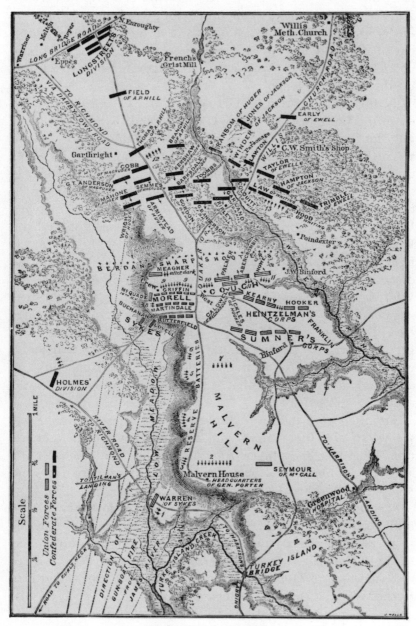

Battle of Malvern Hill

They didn't arrive until noon, however. After they were dispatched, Huger just sat there with his other two brigades, led by Ransom and Mahone, making no attempt to advance. Longstreet finally had to tell him the road in his front was clear and to move out at once. In his report Huger stated he "was much disappointed that General Mahone had not discovered the retreat during the night."

By this time Jackson had crossed White Oak Swamp, come down the Long Bridge road to Glendale, and then turned south into the Quaker road. Consequently, when Ransom and Mahone reached the crossroads they immediately ran into Jackson's troops, causing a bottleneck and slowing up the whole movement. Lee, who was on the Quaker road near Willis Church, then ordered Jackson into position. Jackson formed his line with Whiting's division on his left in the woods and fields around the Poindexter farm east of the Quaker road, and D. H. Hill on his right in the woods west of the road. Ewell's division, with the exception of Taylor's brigade which filled the interval between Whiting and Hill, and all of Jackson's division were in the rear in reserve near Willis Church. Lee then wanted to put Magruder on Hill's right, but as Magruder was not yet up he ordered Huger's two brigades, Ransom's and Mahone's, into position there, with Magruder to form on their right when he came up. Lee apparently did not realize that Huger had already sent Armistead and Wright into that area.

Trying to work their way through Jackson's reserve troops and the woods and the swamps, and receiving contradictory orders from Magruder and Huger, Ransom and his men reached their assigned position in the line just before dark; and by the time Mahone reached his, the battle had already started.

Magruder, it will be recalled, had been sent down the Darbytown road after the affair at Savage Station on June 28, and had spent the night in a fruitless march. The next day, during the battle of Glendale, Lee had ordered him down the New Market road to support Holmes. Darkness came on before Magruder reached Holmes, however, much to Longstreet's and Lee's disgust; so Lee then ordered him back to Glendale to relieve Longstreet's troops in the line after the battle had ceased. Now Lee ordered him to take a road that would put him in position on Jackson's right at Malvern Hill. Unfortunately, however, through a misunderstanding over which road actually was the Quaker road, Magruder proceeded in the wrong direction. Then Longstreet galloped up in person and convinced Magruder to take another road putting him close to Jackson's right. When he reached the area, of course, he found it filled with Huger's troops, but he finally got into position behind Armistead and Wright on Lee's extreme right flank. By this time it was five o'clock. Longstreet and A. P. Hill, their ranks decimated by the actions at Gaines's Mill and Glendale, were held in reserve on the Long Bridge road. Lee stated in his report, "Owing to ignorance of the country, the dense forests impeding necessary communication, and the extreme difficulty of the ground, the whole line was not formed until a late hour in the afternoon."

The day had certainly started badly for Lee and it got worse before it ended. There seems to have been some disagreement among Lee and his commanders as to how the battle should be fought. D. H. Hill was convinced that the Federal position was too strong to be attacked. "If General McClellan is there in force," he told Lee, "we had better let him alone." Longstreet scoffed and replied, "Don't get scared, now that we have got him whipped." Jackson apparently did not want a frontal assault, but suggested an attempt to turn the Federal right. Longstreet, however, insisted that he had found a "position offering good play for batteries across the Federal left" and suggested that sixty pieces from there playing on the enemy would do such damage as to warrant an assault by infantry, provided Jackson could get enough guns in his front into action so that an effective crossfire could be brought to bear.

In theory this was practical, but in fact it was impossible to carry out. The topography alone would be enough to prevent its execution, as any proper reconnaissance would have shown, without even considering the fact that Porter's artillery was already in position and could quickly cut those guns to pieces one by one as they tried to unlimber for any attack. Nevertheless, Lee seemed to feel that this might be his last chance to destroy McClellan's army; so with this idea in mind he issued his orders.

The plan of battle—if indeed it can be called that—was for Armistead, on Lee's right, to charge with a yell after the massed Confederate artillery had blasted a hole in the Federal line. As a "battle order" this was almost unbelievable. In the first place, it put the responsibility of where and when to begin the attack on a mere brigade commander. In the second place, Armistead commanded but one of fourteen brigades ordered to attack, extending over a mile in densely wooded country and all under heavy enemy artillery fire. Any one of them, simply by changing position to escape the hail of lead and iron, could inadvertently give the signal for the assault without meaning to. Also, it would be impossible, with the noise, smoke, and confusion, for all these brigades to act in concert from such a signal.

Even worse than that, however, is the fact that no orders or instructions were given to General Pendleton's reserve artillery, to which belonged the heavy-caliber guns that would be needed for such a plan. Pendleton stated in his report: "Tuesday morning, July 1, was spent by me in seeking for some time the commanding general, that I might get orders and . . . in examining positions near the two armies, toward ascertaining . . . whether any position could be reached whence our large guns might be used to good purpose . . . no site was found from which the large guns could play upon the enemy without endangering our own troops. . . ."

This, of course, left only the divisional field batteries in operation, and it was too late when Lee realized that they could not be brought into effective play. After the war Longstreet belatedly admitted that "the ground over which our batteries were to pass into position on our right was so rough and obstructed that of the artillery ordered for use there only one or two batteries could go in at a time," and the Federals "tore them into fragments in a few minutes after they opened, piling horses upon each other, and guns upon horses." It was unfortunate that he hadn't discovered the fact before he offered his idea to Lee.

Armistead, undoubtedly worried about the grave responsibility resting on his shoulders, requested artillery for his front; and Pegram's and Grimes's batteries were sent to him. They were quickly cut to pieces and entirely disabled, however. D. H. Hill, on the left, fared no better, each battery being knocked out as soon as it came up; but, apparently thinking the action in front of Armistead was the signal, Hill attacked, thus bringing on the battle. Alone and unsupported on either flank, Hill ran into Couch's right and Kearny's left and was driven back with heavy losses. He requested reinforcements. Jackson ordered up his own division and Ewell's, waiting around Willis Church on the Quaker road, but they got lost in the swamps, woods, and tanglefoot underbrush and didn't reach Hill until after dark.

By now Magruder was up, behind Wright and Armistead, and before Mahone or Ransom were in position he ordered an assault, despite the fact that Armistead had not charged at all, being pinned down by the Federal artillery. As was to be expected, the attack when it came was piecemeal and uncoordinated as first Wright and Armistead advanced against Morell's front and were beaten back, and then Semmes, Kershaw, Mahone, and Cobb tried it.

At the sound of the yelled orders the men sprang forward. It was a blind and hopeless rush by a collection of regiments in

Federal Artillery at Malvern Hill

dusty and tattered gray, out of the woods, up the slope, toward the exploding fury of the belching cannon. Then musketry fire went out to meet the charging wave. Many of the gray shapes went down; others charged on. The wave, its front now uneven, flowed up the rising ground almost to the cannon muzzles before it finally broke in the hollow beneath the ridge and ebbed back toward the shelter of the trees. At that, the Federal line had almost been pierced momentarily in one spot by the Third Georgia of Wright's brigade, but the Fourteenth New York quickly rushed in and closed the gap. Wright reported: "The fire was terrific beyond anything I had ever witnessed—indeed the hideous shrieking of shells through the dusky gloom of closing night, the whizzing of bullets, the loud and incessant roll of artillery and small-arms, were enough to make the stoutest heart quail."

It was hopeless and useless, a wanton waste of life, a ghastly mistake. Nothing at all was accomplished by the attack. If it had never been made, the Federal army would still have been withdrawn during the night. The Confederates suffered over 5,000 casualties. Said the caustic D. H. Hill, "It was not war—it was murder."

Lee was not happy with the way the battle was conducted. It seems that sometime after three o'clock, realizing that his artillery could not be concentrated in any one spot in order to blast a hole in the Federal line, he was thinking of abandoning Longstreet's idea and possibly using A. P. Hill's and Longstreet's troops to follow Jackson's suggestion of an attack on the Federal right. But it was already too late, and the orders could not be changed in time to stop D. H. Hill or Magruder from attacking.

An attack on the Federal right probably would not have been any more successful anyway. Although the terrain would have been easier on an attacking force, Sumner and Franklin were both in position there, backed by plenty of reserve artillery, and by the time Lee could have made the move it would have been dusk. In his report Lee stated: "The obstacles presented by the woods and swamp made it impracticable to bring up a sufficient amount of artillery to oppose successfully the extraordinary force of that arm employed by the enemy, while the field itself afforded us few positions favorable for its use and none for its proper concentration."

Porter, of course, was well satisfied with the day's results. Although there had been little movement or guidance during the battle, with the exception of a few regiments and brigades and some siege artillery, the position selected and the disposition of troops and artillery were certainly a credit to the officers involved. And now Porter suggested to McClellan that they hold this powerful position, even if they didn't advance on Richmond. McClellan, on board a gunboat on the James, sent Porter his answer at 9 P.M. "The General Commanding desires you to move your command at once, the artillery reserve moving first to Harrison's Bar."

The Seven Days were over, "seven days of smoke and noise, and heat, and bloodshed, and wounds, and groans, and sufferings, mingled with loud huzzas and rejoicings," as one veteran described them. And now a sad silence settled momentarily over Malvern Hill, broken only by the pitiful cries of the wounded and the dying. "I have never seen a battlefield," wrote an officer after the war, "where there was such frightful mutilation of bodies as there was at Malvern Hill, owing to so much artillery having been used. Many were cut entirely in two. Some were headless, while fragments of bodies and limbs were strewn about in every direction." In the dark, somber woods, in the filthy, stinking swamps, the surgeons were busily amputating in the eerie glow of lanterns under the long black shadows.

The Judgment
of History:
McClellan's Failure

In the early morning darkness of July 2 a sullen rain set in, wrapping Malvern Hill in a ghostly mist. The drops ticked off the leaves with the steady inexorable sound of eternity as the weary Federal soldiers prepared to start yet another session of stumbling through the dark, the rain, and the mud. Dispirited, hungry, and haggard, most of them were worn out from marching rather than fighting. They huddled together silently, their patched and faded uniforms smeared with the red-clayish Virginia mud that stuck like glue. From the surrounding blackness the soul-searing moans of the wounded echoed hauntingly through the motionless trees. The pungent odor from the heat-bloated bodies of dead men and horses was stifling.

And yet most of them realized a great victory had been won, and would have willingly marched toward Richmond rather than away from it. "The order to go forward and seek our rations in Richmond would have been received with wild enthusiasm," one veteran insisted. Even the general officers were not immune to this belief. Although Porter merely wanted to maintain his position, others, particularly Kearny and "Fighting Joe" Hooker, desired an immediate advance on the Confederate capital. Kearny, who had lost an arm in Mexico, was almost vehement about the order to withdraw. "I say to you all," he shouted, "such an order can only be prompted by cowardice or treason."

Holding the position at Malvern Hill was one thing, but advancing on Richmond at this stage of the campaign was another problem entirely. The Army of the Potomac was near exhaustion; many of the men were without rations and short on ammunition; stragglers were numerous, most of them minus their muskets; no organized line of supply existed; and, more important, no plans were available for such a movement. Under the circumstances, only two courses were practical: hold or retreat to the James. McClellan chose the latter as he believed his men were "wornout by fighting every day and marching every night for a week." Also, and more important, he was anxious for the protection the gunboats offered. When he ordered Porter to withdraw, he informed Washington: "If possible I shall retire tonight to Harrison's Bar where the gunboats can render more aid in covering our position. More gunboats are much needed."

So all through the dismal night the tired regiments marched the last eight muddy miles to Harrison's Landing on the James, guided by fires hissing and sputtering in the rain. Slocum's division of Franklin's corps led off, with Keyes's Fourth Corps acting as the main rear guard. The cavalry, wagons, and artillery kept to the roads, churning them into troughs of liquid mud. One soldier insisted he saw a mule disappear into a mud hole up to its ears, although he admitted that it might have been a small mule. The infantry generally kept to the woods and fields, sloshing along slowly in the muck. A veteran of the Nineteenth Massachusetts recalled that this march "from Malvern Hill to Harrison's Landing was one of the worst the regiment ever experienced. The men pulled and struggled along through the mud in the darkness, drenched to the skin. . . . When daylight appeared, it

The Road to Harrison's Landing

revealed hundreds of men by the roadside who had become exhausted and left behind by their regiments."

Porter selected Colonel Averell's Third Pennsylvania Cavalry, supported by Buchanan's brigade of regulars from Sykes's division and one battery, to act as rear guard for his withdrawal. At daybreak Averell lined his men up on the crest of the hill in back of the Crew house, and as the first yellow rays of the morning sun shifted the gray mist a horrible scene unfolded before their eyes. "Over five thousand dead and wounded men were on the ground," Averell reported, "in every attitude of distress. A third of them were dead or dying, but enough were alive and moving to give to the field a singular crawling effect."

When the battery assigned to him was late in reporting, Averell utilized one of his squadrons, organized into squads, to give the appearance of a battery unlimbering for action. They skipped about in the mist in sections, creating the illusion of placing guns in strategic spots, until the rear battery showed up. But the only Confederate to advance up the hill was a lone officer carrying a white flag and requesting a truce to bury the dead and pick up the wounded. Technically, Averell did not have the authority to grant such a truce, but as his mission was to protect the withdrawal by gaining time, he readily consented. By ten o'clock, when the truce expired, the main part of the Federal army was at

Harrison's Landing and the remaining wagons safely on their way there. Under cover of another heavy rainstorm, Averell then withdrew and joined Keyes's corps, several miles to the rear.

Although McClellan and Porter made much of Averell's actions in their reports, the fact is that the Confederate forces were in no condition to conduct a vigorous pursuit of the retreating Federals. Most of the brigades involved in the abortive assault of the previous day had been literally cut to pieces. The ground over which they would have to advance was littered with their own dead and wounded. The various commands, with the exception of Longstreet's and A. P. Hill's, which had been held in reserve, were completely disorganized and in many cases demoralized. One soldier remembered that after Malvern Hill they were "tired, worn-out, disgusted, and with nothing to eat." Magruder's and Huger's troops were so inextricably mixed that it took two days to straighten them out. General Trimble, of Ewell's command, reported that he "found the whole army in the utmost disorder—thousands of straggling men asking every passer-by for their regiments; ambulances, wagons, and artillery obstructing every road, and altogether, in a drenching rain, presenting a scene of the utmost woeful and disheartening confusion."

Lee did issue orders for Jackson and Longstreet to take up the pursuit, with Stuart's cavalry in the lead, but by the time the orders were given and the commands organized the heavy rainstorm made marching almost impossible. Lee and Davis, on the field as usual, finally agreed that the condition of the army and the weather prohibited any further effort that day. This was just as well, because it took Jackson all day to get his command organized to march, and Longstreet made only two miles the whole day.

Stuart's situation was something else again, however. After spending all day June 29 rationing his command from the Federal delicacies abandoned at White House, he had been ordered by Lee to continue to watch the bridges lower down the Chickahominy in case McClellan headed for the York rather than the James. It was not until the night of June 30, after the battle of Glendale, that Lee finally ordered him to rejoin the Army of

Northern Virginia, and then the order was vague and couched in general terms—as indeed were most of Lee's orders during this period. To a man like Stuart, this was an open invitation to take whatever action pleased him. His orders read merely to cross the Chickahominy, suggesting but not ordering, Grapevine Bridge, and cooperate with Jackson. Although Lee wrote the order at 9 P.M., Stuart did not receive it until 3:30 the next morning, that is, July 1. And then, instead of ascertaining Jackson's position and requesting orders, on the basis of his own analysis of the situation he started out for Bottom's Bridge, eleven miles away. Crossing the Chickahominy there, he proceeded to White Oak Swamp, where he discovered the roads so choked with ambulances, wagons, and artillery trains that it was impossible for his command to proceed. Retracing his steps to Bottom's Bridge, he then led his command farther down the river and recrossed at Forge Bridge, still with no idea of Jackson's whereabouts, and headed in the general direction of Malvern Hill. It was now dark, the battle was over, and the weary troopers had ridden a total of forty-two miles without accomplishing anything.

Stuart, however, never one to underestimate his own importance or to let his actions pass unnoticed if he could help it, pompously reported: "My arrival could not have been more fortunately timed, for, arriving after dark, its ponderous march, with the rolling artillery, must have impressed the enemy's cavalry, watching the approaches to their rear, with the idea of an immense army about to cut off their retreat, and contributed to cause that sudden collapse and stampede that soon after occurred, leaving us in possession of Malvern Hill, which the enemy might have held next day much to our detriment." The fact was the Federals didn't even know Stuart was there.

Finally, the next morning, Stuart located Jackson and, after receiving his orders, took off after the enemy columns, long after Averell's cavalry had withdrawn. The day was spent collecting stragglers and discarded equipment, however, not in intercepting any part of the withdrawal. Late that night, July 2, Stuart sent Captain John Pelham with one 12-pound howitzer and a squad of the First Virginia Cavalry on ahead to reconnoiter McClellan's position.

The young Pelham quickly discovered that McClellan had made a serious blunder in his position at Harrison's Landing. A slightly elevated plateau, called Evelington Heights by the natives, completely commanded the Federal encampment, and McClellan had neglected to fortify it. Pelham immediately realized that a strong artillery force on the Heights could raise havoc with the huge army packed into the relatively small area about the landing. He quickly notified Stuart of the situation and wisely refrained from any further action so as not to alert the Federals to their exposed position.

Stuart sent a dispatch to Jackson and then, typically, took off without orders to take personal charge of the situation. Finding only a squadron of cavalry in his way, he quickly seized the Heights the next morning, and then, incredibly, he opened up on the whole Army of the Potomac with his one lone howitzer rather than waiting for the arrival of Jackson and Longstreet. The sudden booming of the howitzer, as Stuart reported, caused great excitement among the soldiers in blue and undoubtedly gave Stuart and his troopers a good laugh, but that was all it gave them. When the Federal infantry quickly advanced against him, Stuart was forced to withdraw, losing for Lee an excellent opportunity to inflict heavy damage to the Army of the Potomac. By the time Longstreet arrived that night and Jackson the next morning, the Heights were heavily fortified and practically impregnable. After a personal examination later that day Lee decided the position was too strong to be attacked, particularly as any attacking force would necessarily come under the range of the Federal gunboats on the river, and wisely withdrew. By July 8 the Army of Northern Virginia, with the exception of cavalry outposts and pickets, was back in the camps around Richmond for a much needed rest and reorganization.

In his official report of the campaign, which he postponed writing for two years, Lee stated: "Under ordinary circumstances the Federal Army should have been destroyed." The fact that it wasn't he attributed primarily to "the want of correct and timely information," due to the character of the country and the lack of adequate maps. Characteristically, he did not attempt to place any of the blame for the failure on any of his subordinates, or on his government. Neither did he overlook what had been accomplished. "The siege of Richmond was raised, and the object of a campaign, which had been prosecuted after months of preparation at an enormous expenditure of men and money, completely frustrated."

What Lee meant by "ordinary circumstances," however, is certainly not clear. It may be that, writing two years after the event, he was thinking in terms of what he and his commanders and the Army of Northern Virginia would have done *then* under the same conditions. If so, it was a more or less meaningless statement, because two years later the Federal army and its commanders had also changed and developed from experience. Possessing adequate maps may be considered an ordinary circumstance for any army in the field, to be sure, but correct maps would not have helped Jackson to rebuild Grapevine Bridge or to cross White Oak Swamp any quicker than he did; nor would they have made Huger and Magruder any more aggressive, and they would not have helped Lee to decide whether McClellan was retreating to the York or the James. What was needed even more than good maps was competent staff work, explicit battle orders, and simple, rather than complicated, maneuvers.

In a sense, the Seven Days had been a shake-down cruise, so to speak, for both Lee and the Army of Northern Virginia, and considered in such fashion it must be regarded as a Confederate success, despite all the mistakes and lost opportunities. Lee's reputation was now an established fact, and the war in the east would be entrusted to his direction. It was clear to the other generals that they would have to work in harmony under Lee or not at all, as he had the complete confidence of Davis and the Confederate government and the soldiers who made up the army. All this was a gain, along with the relief of Richmond, to be balanced against the 20,000 casualties suffered in the Seven Days, among them many field- and company-grade officers who would be desperately missed in the years ahead when competent regimental, brigade, and divisional commanders were urgently needed.

In the overall view, Lee showed a firm knowledge of military principles and the lessons learnt from all the campaigns of the great commanders in history, and, more important, he showed he had the moral courage necessary to put this knowledge to good use. One clear lesson from history was that the defensive should never be assumed except as a means of shifting to the offensive under more favorable conditions. From the time he assumed command after the battle of Seven Pines, Lee acted on this principle. And his plan for the offensive encompassed Napoleon's axiom of using a fixed point as a pivot for maneuvering in order to mass superior power at your opponent's weak point. Leaving Huger and Magruder in front of Richmond as the pivot, Lee swung the remainder of his army around by his left to strike McClellan's weak point north of the Chickahominy.

For any plan to succeed, however, it has to be well prepared, carefully directed, correctly timed, and if at all possible, a surprise to the enemy. Although Lee strove for surprise, McClellan was aware of Jackson's approach; so that element was lost. Then, too, A. P. Hill's premature advance on Mechanicsville not only upset the timing, it also deprived Lee of the opportunity to properly direct the succeeding events. Despite these failures, when Lee decided to continue with the plan rather than alter or discard it completely, he showed a rare example of moral courage at its highest degree. Another man might well have hesitated, even though it was a well-known military principle that to vacillate between two plans was worse than to have no plan at all. But, unfortunately for Lee, a good plan and moral courage were not enough.

The preparation, timing, and direction of a plan, even when based on sound military principles, are still dependent on correct interpretation of the enemy's intentions, and here Lee failed. When he assumed that McClellan would withdraw to White House or Yorktown rather than the James River, his whole plan of action was based on a false premise, resulting in 8,000 casualties at Gaines's Mill and achieving nothing. Had he realized what McClellan was planning, the battle of Gaines's Mill probably would not have been fought, or if it had, it would not have been on such a large scale.

When Lee finally interpreted McClellan's intentions correctly, of course, he needed a new plan. But even before this new plan was formulated the important time element had already been lost through hesitation and delay. And the strategy of converging columns on the crossroads at Glendale, although it looked good on paper, was practically impossible to execute, ignoring as it did the military principle that to attempt to strike a central force by converging columns was almost always fatal to the assailants. General Abner Doubleday, writing of a different battle, expressed it this way: "Let us suppose an army holds the junction of six roads. It seems theoretically plausible that different detachments encircling it, by all attacking at the same time, must confuse and overpower it; but in practice the idea is rarely realized, for no two routes are precisely alike, the columns never move simultaneously, and therefore never arrive at the same time. Some of this is due to the character of the commanders. One man is full of dash, and goes forward at once; another is timid, or at least overcautious, and advances slowly; a third stops to recall some outlying detachments, or to make elaborate preparations. The result is, the outer army has lost its strength and is always beaten in detail. One portion is sure to be defeated before the others arrive." That is exactly what happened to Lee at Savage Station and Glendale. Before the advent of modern communications made perfect synchronization possible, this strategy was always dangerous, even with perfect staff work.

Malvern Hill, of course, was a complete Confederate blunder, apparently based on desperation and frustration. In the military sense, strategy is the art of bringing the enemy to battle on terms advantageous to yourself and disadvantageous to him. At Malvern Hill this worked in the exact reverse for Lee. And the tactics decided upon, to blast a hole in the Federal line with artillery, were impossible to execute. Effective tactics required coordination between the infantry, artillery, and cavalry, and the only one who could ensure this coordination was the supreme commander. Without it even the most brilliant strategy would probably fail. In this battle Lee's strategy was poor and his tactics unsound.

Mistakes, however, are common to all generals and all battles. Even the great Napoleon was not immune. The important thing was that Lee, despite the mistakes, had proved himself a competent and daring field commander who would learn from experience. And now that the immediate threat to Richmond had been removed, he wanted to shift the area of conflict as far from the Confederate capital as possible. He wrote to Jefferson Davis: "If we are able to change the theater of war from the James River to the north of the Rappahannock we shall be able to consume provisions and forage now being used in supporting the enemy."

Not for another two years would the Army of Northern Virginia and the Army of the Potomac clash again in the outskirts of Richmond. Lee saw to that. And the army was ready for whatever task, no matter how formidable, Lee would give it. Although fatigued and disorganized after the arduous Seven Days, a few weeks in the camps around Richmond found the men ready and willing for whatever the future might hold. They had found the right man to lead them, and they would follow to the bitter end. As a young Georgian wrote home: "I have seen, heard and felt many things in the last week that I never want to see, hear nor feel again, but these are the lot of life."

The men in the Army of the Potomac were also fatigued and, to some extent at least, demoralized, despite the fact that Malvern Hill had been their greatest victory of the Seven Days. They had marched too many nights in the dark and the rain, had seen too many supplies put to the torch, to be convinced that this was just a change of base and not a retreat. They had lost 52 pieces of artillery (although McClellan never would admit it) and 35,000 small arms, most of the latter discarded by men either too tired or too disgusted to care. They realized they had never been put into action as an army at any time during the Seven Days. Most of them had been more than anxious to help their comrades in the Fifth Corps at Gaines's Mill, but the orders were never given, and in every other action they were used only piecemeal. However, the 15,000 casualties suffered spoke well for their fighting ability, as it represented only a 10 percent loss as compared to 22 percent for the Army of Northern Virginia. It was to be expected, of course, that an attacking force would sustain more casualties than the defenders.

But, like their counterparts in gray, after a few days' rest and some hot food they were ready to go forward again. And despite

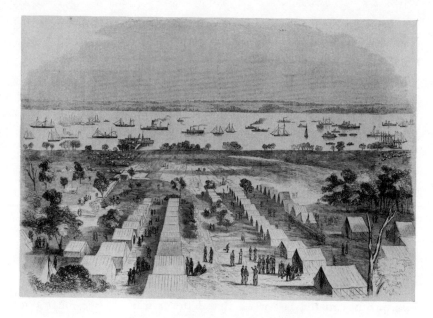

Federal Camp, Harrison's Landing

the heavy losses in supplies and equipment, Quartermaster General Ingalls could report by July 20 that the army still had 3,100 wagons, 350 ambulances, 7,000 cavalry horses, 5,000 artillery horses, and 5,000 team horses, in addition to 8,000 mules. "Upon the river was a large fleet of transports, having on board an abundance of supplies of all kinds. The army was then perfectly equipped so far as I observed, and was in condition to move forward."

Unfortunately, this was just the quartermaster's opinion, not McClellan's. The previous July, when he had assumed command in Washington, McClellan had written derisively, "I found no army to command . . . a mere collection of regiments cowering on the banks of the Potomac." Now he had an army that was ready, willing, and able to fight, but instead he kept it cowering on the banks of the James. All he wanted to be ready to move forward was another 100,000 men, more or less. "To accomplish the great task of capturing Richmond and putting an end to this rebellion," he telegraphed Washington on July 3, "re-enforcements should be sent to me rather much over than much less than

Unloading of Fresh Supplies at Harrison's Landing

100,000 men." Two days earlier, on July 1, he would have settled for 50,000 if sent "promptly"; but when they didn't arrive in two days, his needs had doubled. This, of course, was typical of McClellan. And there can be little doubt that even if the 50,000 had arrived he would have needed another 50,000 in a few days anyway.

Lincoln himself answered the first request, showing amazing patience with his general, even though he did word it as if he were addressing a child. "Your dispatch of Tuesday morning induces me to hope your army is having some rest. In this hope allow me to reason with you a moment. When you ask for 50,000 men to be promptly sent you, you surely labor under some gross mistake of fact. Recently you sent papers showing your disposal of forces made last spring for the defense of Washington and advising a return to that plan. I find it included in and about Washington 75,000 men. Now, please be assured I have not men enough to fill that very plan by 15,000. All of Fremont's in the valley, all of Banks's, all of McDowell's not with you, and all in Washington, taken together, do not exceed, if they reach, 60,000.

With Wool and Dix added to those mentioned I have not, outside of your army, 75,000 men east of the mountains. Thus the
idea of sending you 50,000, or any other considerable force,
promptly is simply absurd."

McClellan undoubtedly knew all that well enough, or should
have, but he also knew that Halleck had a large army west of the
mountains. Even before the Seven Days he had advanced the
ridiculous idea that his army be strengthened at the expense of
Halleck's forces, not because of any real need but simply because
their presence would have a great "moral" effect. It is no doubt
true that McClellan never did appreciate the importance of the
strategy in the west—in one of his letters he stated the western
action would be a "mere bagatelle"—obsessed as he was with the
idea of capturing Richmond. The fact that the war would ultimately be won and lost in the west was something he failed completely to comprehend. But this by itself does not fully explain
his attempts to build up the Army of the Potomac at the expense
of all other forces. It is more than possible that McClellan had an
ulterior motive also. He was thoroughly imbued with the European idea of a powerful military leader conducting campaigns
without interference from royalty or government. When he had
hesitated in front of Yorktown early in April, Lincoln. had telegraphed: "I think you had better break the enemy's line from
Yorktown to Warwick at once." McClellan immediately informed his wife, "I was much tempted to reply that he had better
come and do it himself," and then quoted an example of a European general who had done just that to his government during
the Crimean War while McClellan had been serving as an observer. The idea seemed to be that if he could build up his army
to 300,000 or more, thus in his mind making himself the most
powerful general in the country, he would then be in a position
to tell the president and the government what he intended to do
and when, whether they liked it or not. And if they didn't like it
he could, in a sense, tell them to come and do it themselves. All
of this, of course, based on the premise that he would be too
powerful and too popular with the troops and the public for the
government to remove him from command.

The only answer to the telegram the president received was

McClellan's request to Stanton for more than 100,000 troops. It was becoming increasingly apparent that McClellan was not a man you could reason with. Fortunately, however, Lincoln never lost his intelligent grasp of the situation as a whole. Even before Malvern Hill, when communication with McClellan was still disrupted, he had requested Halleck to ship 25,000 troops east if possible, but not if it would endanger the chances for success in the west. He stated clearly, "To take and hold the railroad at or east of Cleveland, in east Tennessee, I think fully as important as the taking and holding of Richmond." But when McClellan came up with his unreasonable demands, Lincoln canceled his order to Halleck. If McClellan was not going to be satisfied with less than 100,000 men, there would be no point in weakening the western force to ship him a mere 25,000.

A noted military authority has stated that if a commanding general "considers the means placed at his disposal inadequate he need not accept the position offered him, but he steps beyond his province as a strategist if he attempts to dictate to the government what, in the widest sense, the means supplied to him should be." McClellan, however, did not believe it was beyond his province, nor did he have any intention of resigning, despite his statement to his wife that he had "no faith in the administration, and shall cut loose from public life the very moment my country can dispense with my services." Instead, he sent General Marcy, his father-in-law and chief of staff, to Washington to plead his case for him.

Marcy, however, made the mistake of overstating the case, strongly implying that if McClellan did not receive the reinforcements he requested the army might be forced to capitulate. The mere mention of capitulation made the nervous Stanton suspect treason, and it profoundly shocked the president when he heard about it. "General," he told Marcy sternly, "I understand you have used the word 'capitulate'; that is a word not to be used in connection with our army." The flustered Marcy quickly apologized, but the harm had been done. Lincoln decided to pay a visit to the Army of the Potomac to see for himself what the situation really was. If he found that a feeling of capitulation was in the air and was not just an arrogant threat on McClellan's part to get more men, then McClellan would have to go, and quickly. Lincoln had no intention of quitting the war, nor of allowing anyone else to force him to quit it if he could possibly help it. A few days earlier he had written various state governors that his intentions about the conduct of the war had not changed, despite the recent setback on the peninsula. "I expect to maintain this contest," he told them, "until successful, or till I die, or am conquered, or my term expires, or Congress or the country forsake me."

On the long journey down to the peninsula there were many things on the president's mind. Foremost among them was the question of slavery and what to do about it. Lincoln's position had always been clear on this subject. As he wrote to Horace Greeley, editor of the New York *Tribune*: "My paramount object in this struggle is to save the Union, and is not either to save or destroy slavery. If I could save the Union without freeing any slave, I would do it; and if I could save it by freeing all the slaves, I would do it; and if I could save it by freeing some and leaving others alone, I would also do that." So far he had done nothing directly either for or against slavery, but McClellan's failure assured the nation of a long, bitter war, and the pressures on Lincoln were multiplying. The border states had rejected his offer of compensated emancipation; the failure of the peninsula campaign gave new encouragement to the European powers who desired to aid the South for their own purposes; the Congress was demanding an end to the so-called "kid-glove" treatment of the Rebels and their property; all of which could very definitely affect the saving of the Union, as Lincoln saw it. As he later told a White House visitor: "Things had gone from bad to worse, until I felt that we had reached the end of our rope on the plan of operations we had been pursuing; that we had about played our last card, and must change our tactics, or lose the game." In other words, he had just about decided that abolition was now necessary for the successful prosecution of the war. Although this action would be based primarily on military, political, and diplomatic considerations, it would also inject a new moral issue into the conflict and thus strongly discourage European intervention.

Lincoln Reviewing Troops at Harrison's Landing

It was in this frame of mind that Lincoln reviewed the Army of the Potomac on July 8, and was pleasantly surprised to find that it was not a beaten army at all; only its commanding general had been defeated. McClellan wrote to his wife about this visit. "He found the army anything but demoralized or dispirited; in excellent spirits. I do not know to what extent he has profited by his visit; not much, I fear." But Little Mac was mistaken; Lincoln had learned a great deal. Not, however, about any new plans for fighting the Army of Northern Virginia or capturing Richmond. What he did learn was more about the character of his general.

The first thing McClellan did when the president reached the peninsula was to hand him his famous Harrison Bar letter. Lincoln read it, put it in his pocket, and never mentioned it again. The forbearance the president showed on this occasion was truly amazing. The letter was nothing more than a pompous statement of McClellan's political beliefs, which he generously admitted did not "relate to the situation of this army or strictly come within the scope of my official duties." He then went on to state categorically: "Neither confiscation of property, political executions of persons, territorial organization of States, or forcible abolition of slavery should be contemplated for a moment. . . . A declaration of radical views, especially upon slavery, will rapidly disintegrate our present armies."

McClellan apparently had not changed any since he left Washington. He was still more interested in politics than in fighting the war. And his presumption in handing the president such a document, after the failure of his campaign involving a large expenditure of men and money, can only be explained in terms of McClellan's egotistical belief that he was far superior to the president in every way and was fairly confident, even at this early date, of securing the Democratic presidential nomination in 1864.

The president also learned something else. Early in April he had relieved McClellan as commanding general of all the armies so that he could concentrate on the peninsula campaign alone, and since then the president had acted more or less as his own commander in chief. This had upset McClellan as he had worked very diligently to undermine old General Scott and secure the position for himself, and ever since he had been insisting to Washington that someone be appointed to fill the vacancy—preferably himself, of course. Lincoln had also concluded by now that he needed someone; but if McClellan had not already eliminated himself from consideration, he definitely did with this letter. In it he naïvely informed the president that this commander in chief should be "one who possesses your confidence, understands your views, and who is competent to execute your orders by directing the military of the nation to the accomplishment of the objects by you proposed." At the same time he informed his wife, "I do not know what paltry trick the administration will play next." By thought, word, and deed, McClellan had proved that he was definitely not the man for the job.

Shortly after his return to Washington Lincoln appointed General Halleck his new commander in chief, much to McClellan's disgust. "I cannot remain permanently in the army after this slight," he told his wife. "It is grating to have to serve under the orders of a man whom I know by experience to be my inferior." Then he added, "I am tired of serving fools." This, of course, could mean only Lincoln and Stanton. Not only did McClellan feel that he was the best qualified man for the presidency, he also regarded himself as the greatest general in the country, although a much persecuted one. "The present feeling," he stated, "is merely a continuation of the inveterate persecution that has pursued me since I landed on the Peninsula. . . . The game apparently is to deprive me of the means of moving, and then to cut off my head for not advancing." These words are in shocking contrast to Lincoln's statement: "I shall do nothing through malice; what I deal with is too vast for malice."

Halleck lost no time in visiting McClellan and the Army of the Potomac. A difficult decision had to be made, and soon: whether to make another attempt at Richmond from the line of the James, or to publicly admit the campaign was a failure and withdraw the army to Washington to start out again on a new line. Halleck was authorized to promise McClellan not more than an additional 20,000 men. If Richmond could be attacked with a reasonable chance for success with these reinforcements, the president would agree to it; otherwise the army would be withdrawn. McClellan requested 30,000 troops, still insisting that Lee had at least 200,000 men; but when Halleck reiterated that he could promise only 20,000, McClellan reluctantly agreed that there might be a "chance" and was "willing to try it." This was not good enough.

Shortly after his return to Washington Halleck sent McClellan a long dispatch in which he stated that the decision had been made to withdraw the army and explained why. "You and your officers at one interview estimated the enemy's forces in and around Richmond at 200,000 men. . . . General Pope's army covering Washington is only about 40,000. Your effective force is only about 90,000. You are 30 miles from Richmond, and General Pope 80 or 90, with the enemy directly between you, ready to fall with his superior numbers upon one or the other, as he may elect. Neither can re-enforce the other in case of such an attack. . . . In other words, the old Army of the Potomac is split into two parts . . . and I wish to unite them."

Right or wrong, the thing was done. In August the Army of the Potomac was transported by water back to Washington to support Pope's campaign in northern Virginia.

Under the circumstances, it is difficult to see how any other decision could have been made. McClellan might have started to march on Richmond again but there can be little doubt that it soon would have been the same old refrain again of needing more men. At the rate he was estimating Lee's forces he would have them up to 250,000 in a short time, necessitating more delay. And there is no reason to suppose that McClellan would change his strategy of regular approaches and siege tactics. It is even conceivable that Lee could have left a small holding force in front of McClellan, marched the bulk of his army north to overwhelm Pope, and then return quickly to handle McClellan. This would mean that 150,000 Federal troops would be tied up along the banks of the James accomplishing absolutely nothing.

The point is, McClellan had no intention or desire to fight. His whole philosophy of military operations was summed up in an earlier letter to his wife. "No prospect of a brilliant victory shall induce me to depart from my intention of gaining success by maneuvering rather than by fighting." This, basically, is the answer to McClellan's whole peninsula campaign. Imbued with the old European idea of maneuvering, he believed that the general who best husbanded his reserves and ended a campaign with the most men was the victor. This had been true, to a certain extent, with the professional armies of Europe when it was an expensive proposition to replace lost men, but McClellan was not dealing with professional soldiers. This was a civil war involving citizen soldiers, and one side would have to destroy the other before it would end, and to do that great risks would have to be taken. An editorial in *Harper's Weekly* noted: "Doubtless the Government knows that it must be vigorous; but does it sufficiently remember that *risk* is essential to vigor? If it can not take risks, the rebels can and will."

Lincoln understood this from the beginning, as well as the fact that the old methods would no longer work. As he stated to Congress: "The dogmas of the quiet past are inadequate to the stormy present. As our case is new so we must think anew and act anew." This, however, was something McClellan was incapable of doing. The war would drag on until the president found generals who could think and act anew.

The conclusion is inescapable that McClellan was a failure as a field commander in the peninsula campaign. Some apologists have tried to screen this failure by pointing to the brilliant logistical work involved in the change of base. This thesis, of course, conveniently ignores the fact that McClellan's mission was to defeat the Army of Northern Virginia and capture Richmond. It also ignores the fact that the necessity for the change of base was caused by McClellan's faulty disposition of troops from the beginning, and the fact that the change, if it was going to be made at all, should have been made in May after the destruction of the *Merrimac* and the fall of Norfolk opened the James to within seven miles of Richmond. And if McClellan can be credited with the successful logistics, he certainly cannot be given credit for any of the battles fought during the maneuver; he wasn't even on the field.

Under this philosophy of maneuvering rather than fighting, of course, in McClellan's mind it was not necessary for him to be on the battlefield; he had to direct the maneuver, which was more important than any battle so far as he was concerned. But it is a military truism that even on the defensive a good commander will always be seeking to discover where he can strike the most effective blow. If McClellan had been a good commander, the Army of Northern Virginia might have been destroyed at Gaines's Mill. But a good commander needs moral courage above all, and in this McClellan was sadly lacking, despite the bravado he tried to show in his report with the statement: "To the calm judgment of history and the future I leave the task of pronouncing upon this movement, confident that its verdict will be that no such difficult movement was ever more successfully executed; that no army ever fought more repeatedly, heroically, and successfully against great odds. . . ."

It is noteworthy that the only thing Little Mac wanted to leave to the "calm judgment of history" was his change of base, not his record against the Army of Northern Virginia or his mission to capture Richmond. On this point he felt safe because he had filled the records with documents that concealed his intentions and always stressed the "great odds" against which he was constantly contending. But McClellan was not trained as a historian; in fact, in this respect military training is the exact opposite of the historian's training, as the former fosters the habit of unquestioning obedience, while the latter seeks the truth and always tries to determine the why behind all military decisions. Consequently, while he could fill the official records with reports designed to protect and glorify himself, his actions and letters to his wife revealed his true self to the "calm judgment of history."

And it is very evident that McClellan could not change. When he returned to Washington from Harrison's Landing, his troops were detached from him and sent to Pope; later, when Lee defeated Pope at Second Manassas late in August, the Federal army was once again demoralized and McClellan was called upon once more to restore order and discipline, which he did. But when Lee took advantage of this victory to move north into Maryland, McClellan was slow in following; and although he did stop Lee at Antietam in September, he characteristically failed to follow up the victory with an offensive. Instead, he let the Confederates retreat unmolested. On October 13 Lincoln inquired: "Are you not overcautious when you assume you cannot do what the enemy is constantly doing?" And when McClellan gave the poor condition of his horses as one excuse for not moving, the president telegraphed: "I have read your dispatch about sore-tongued and fatigued horses. Will you pardon me for asking what the horses of your army have done since the battle of Antietam that fatigues anything?"

Finally, late in October, the Army of the Potomac advanced cautiously into Virginia; but the movement was so slow, averaging only five or six miles a day, that Lincoln finally took the drastic step of removing McClellan from command early in November. He was ordered to Trenton, New Jersey to await further orders, which never came. In effect, McClellan had been removed from any further active participation in the war. When Lee heard this, he remarked wryly that he hated to part with Mac because "we always understood each other so well. I fear they may continue to make these changes until they find someone I don't understand."

But if McClellan was not active as a general, he was as a politician. The Democratic convention, meeting in Chicago in August, 1864, adopted a peace plank in its platform and nominated Mc-

Clellan as its presidential candidate. The platform was ingeniously contrived to appeal to all those opposed to Lincoln and the war, but flexible enough to be governed by the military events between then and the election in November. On election day McClellan resigned his commission in the Army, but was soundly defeated, carrying only the three states of New Jersey, Delaware, and Kentucky.

Bitterly disappointed, McClellan spent the next three years abroad. Then, after various executive jobs in the engineering field, he served one term as governor of New Jersey from 1878 to 1881. He died in 1885 at the age of fifty-nine.

Two years later his autobiography was published, entitled *McClellan's Own Story*. On the defensive throughout, the book mostly repeated his original arguments and reports, but it was more revealing than McClellan could have realized or wanted. And the insertion of many of his letters gave to the trained historian of the future the insight so necessary for "the calm judgment of history." The Young Napoleon might better have listened to the words of Lincoln: "Fellow-citizens, we cannot escape history."

A Note on Sources

Most, if not all, of the material used for this study is well known to students of the Civil War. But the Peninsula Campaign, particularly as it saw the emergence of Lee and McClellan, has been generally neglected in recent times. The one indispensable major source, of course, is *War of the Rebellion: A Compilation of the Official Records of the Union and Confederate Armies*, published by the War Department in 1902. All the volumes consulted are in Series I. Despite the extensive use of this source over the years, there is still much unused material available for the careful and patient researcher. For example, the description of McClellan's attempt at peacemaking in this book is taken wholly from the *Official Records* and has not, to the best of the author's knowledge, ever been published elsewhere. Other than that, there is no attempt in this study to present any undiscovered material; rather, what this book attempts to do is to present new interpretations of already known facts, particularly regarding McClellan's character and personality and the reasons for the failure of his campaign. In this regard, another indispensable source is George B. McClellan, *McClellan's Own Story*, New York, 1887. Although completely on the defensive throughout, McClellan unknowingly revealed to the trained historian much more than he probably intended, particularly in his letters to his wife, which often differed from his official reports. In most instances the letters proved to be more truthful.

Other important primary sources used include *Battles and Leaders of the Civil War*, edited by Robert Underwood Johnson and Clarence Clough Buel, 4 vols., New York, 1884–87. This is an excellent compilation of eyewitness reports and participants' accounts of both Federal and Confederate personnel. A similar work is *The Blue and the Gray: The Story of the Civil War as Told by Participants*, edited by Henry Steele Commager, 2 vols., Indianapolis, 1950. Commager's selection emphasizes the life of the soldier and the social aspects behind the lines. An interesting view by an English journalist of events early in the conflict is contained in William Howard Russell, *My Diary North and South*, New York, 1954.

Diaries and personal reminiscences are legion, but the following proved most useful for this study: E. P. Alexander, *Military Memoirs of a Confederate*, New York, 1907; John Beatty, *Memoirs of a Volunteer*, New York, 1946; W. W. Blackford, *War Years with Jeb Stuart*, New York, 1945; S. H. Blackford, *Letters From Lee's Army*, New York, 1947; John D. Billings, *Hardtack and Coffee*, New York, 1887; Sally Brock, *Richmond During the War*, New York, 1867; John O. Cosler, *Four Years in the Stonewall Brigade*, Marietta, 1951; Jacob D. Cox, *Military Reminiscences of the Civil War*, 2 vols., New York, 1900; Mary B. Chesnut, *A Diary From Dixie*, New York, 1905; Joel Cook, *The Siege of Richmond*, Philadelphia, 1862; N. M. Curtis, *From Bull Run to Chancellorsville*, New York, 1906; Jefferson Davis, *The Rise and Fall of the Confederate Government*, 2 vols., New York, 1881; Varina Davis, *Jefferson Davis: A Memoir*, 2 vols., New York, 1890; Charles E. Davis, *Three Years in the Army*, Boston, 1894; Abner Doubleday, *Campaigns of the Civil War*, New York, 1891; George C. Eggleston, *A Rebel's Recollections*, Bloomington, 1959; Warren Goss, *Recollections of a Private*, New York, 1890; John B. Gordon, *Reminiscences of the Civil War*, New York, 1903; John B. Hood, *Advance and Retreat*, New Orleans, 1880; Thomas W. Hyde, *Following the Greek Cross*, Boston, 1894; *History of the Nineteenth Regiment: Massachusetts Volunteers*, Salem, 1906; J. B. Jones, *A Rebel War Clerk's Diary*, 2 vols., Philadelphia, 1866; James Longstreet, *From Manassas to Appomattox*, Philadelphia, 1896; Judith W. McGuire, *Diary of a Southern*

Refugee, Richmond, 1899; Carlton McCarthy, *Detailed Minutiae of Soldier Life*, Richmond, 1882; Carlton McCarthy, *Soldier Life in the Army of Northern Virginia*, Richmond, 1888; John S. Mosby, *Mosby's War Reminiscences*, New York, 1898; William Swinton, *Campaigns of the Army of the Potomac*, New York, 1866; Harold A. Small, editor, *The Road to Richmond*, Berkeley, 1939; Robert Stiles, *Four Years Under Marse Robert*, New York, 1910; *Southern Historical Society Papers*, 47 vols., Richmond, 1876–1930; O. R. Thomson and William H. Rauch, *A History of the Bucktails*, Philadelphia, 1906; Gideon Welles, *The Diary of Gideon Welles*, 3 vols., New York, 1911; John H. Worsham, *One of Jackson's Foot Cavalry*, New York, 1912; Spencer G. Welch, *A Confederate Surgeon's Letters to his Wife*, New York, 1911.

Newspapers proved a valuable source for public opinion and special and social events, particularly the Richmond *Dispatch*; Richmond *Enquirer*; Richmond *Examiner*; New York *Herald*; and New York *Tribune*.

Of the many biographies and general works available, the following were consulted: David H. Bates, *Lincoln in the Telegraph Office*, New York, 1907; Alfred H. Bill, *The Beleaguered City*, New York, 1946; Noah Brooks, *Washington in Lincoln's Time*, New York, 1895; Bruce Catton, *Mr. Lincoln's Army*, New York, 1956; Lenoir Chambers, *Stonewall Jackson*, 2 vols., New York, 1959; Merton E. Coulter, *The Confederate States of America*, Baton Rouge, 1950; R. L. Dabney, *Life and Campaigns of Lt.-Gen. Thomas J. Jackson*, New York, 1866; Clifford Dowdey, *Experiment in Rebellion*, New York, 1946; F. H. Dyer, *A Compendium of the War of the Rebellion*, Des Moines, 1908; H. J. Eckenrode and Bryan Conrad, *George B. McClellan*, Chapel Hill, 1941; Douglas S. Freeman, *R. E. Lee*, 4 vols., New York, 1934; Douglas S. Freeman, *Lee's Lieutenants*, 3 vols., New York, 1945; J. F. C. Fuller, *Decisive Battles of the U.S.A.*, New York, 1942; W. W. Hassler, *A. P. Hill*, Richmond, 1957; W. W. Hassler, *General George B. McClellan*, Baton Rouge, 1957; Thomas Kearny, *General Philip Kearny*, New York, 1937; B. J. Hendrick, *Lincoln's War Cabinet*, Boston, 1946; Margaret Leech, *Reveille in Washington*, New York, 1941; Thomas L. Livermore, *Numbers and Losses in the Civil War*, Boston, 1926; David C. Mearns, *The Lincoln Papers*, 2 vols., New York, 1948; Peter S. Michie, *General McClellan*, New York, 1901; Jay Monaghan, *Diplomat in Carpet Slippers*, New York, 1945; L. C. Pickett, *Pickett and His Men*, Atlanta, 1898; Carl Sandburg, *Abraham Lincoln: The War Years*, 4 vols., New York, 1939; Hudson Strode, *Jefferson Davis: Confederate President*, New York, 1959; Glenn Tucker,

Hancock the Superb, New York, 1960; Kenneth P. Williams, *Lincoln Finds a General*, 2 vols., New York, 1950; T. Harry Williams, *Lincoln and the Radicals*, Madison, 1941; Bell I. Wiley, *The Life of Johnny Reb*, New York, 1943, and *The Life of Billy Yank*, New York, 1951; Jennings C. Wise, *The Long Arm of Lee*, 2 vols., Lynchburg, 1915.

Index

187